OVERCOMING ADVERSITY

WORKBOOK

RICHARD T. CASE

To my wife, Linda, who has walked with me through life—which because we live in the world, we do experience adversity. God gave us understanding of the causes and remedies for adversity, and we have lived them all. Linda has been faithful throughout all these experiences in seeking God, and then having His remedies fulfilled—always. She stands strong throughout and encourages me and others to stay in God's peace and believe that the remedy will be provided—and she is always right—He does provide! It is an honor to be partners with one who has such a wonderful heart: Though we will experience adversity all the days of our lives, we know that we know it will be overcome and we will enjoy God's promised abundant life. She is truly an woman of faith and I have the privilege of walking together in the life and power of God.

Acknowledgments

We wish to thank all of the leaders of our Ministry: **All For Jesus—Living Waters!** These leaders have also learned what it means to live in this world of adversity (we all the time get to have them bear witness to God's faithfulness in overcoming their adversity)—and as they have learned the depth of this critical part of the Christian life, they now are all giving this away to others—who then are learning to have adversity overcome, and thus, it is exponentially multiplying. Thank you all:

These leaders are:

Jake & Mary Beckel
Joe & Leigh Bogar
Rich & Janet Cocchiaro
Larry & Sherry Collet
Scott & Kristen Cornell
David & Melissa Dunkel
Tom & Susanne Ewing
Rick & Kelly Ferris
Joel & Christina Gunn
Scott & Terry Hitchcock
Chris & Jaclyn Hoover
Rick & Nancy Hoover
Tad & Monica Jones
Ed & Becky Kobel
Don & Rachelle Light
Chris and Heidi May
Terry & Josephine Noetzel
Steve & Carolyn Van Ooteghem
Preston & Lynda Pitts
Dan & Kathy Rocconi
Bob & Keri Rockwell
John & Michelle Santaferraro
Allyson & Denny Weinberg
Neal & Kathy Weisenburger

OVERCOMING ADVERSITY
PUBLISHED BY ALL FOR JESUS
7615 Lemon Gulch Way
Castle Rock, CO 80108
www.afjministy.com

ISBN: 978-1-7360588-6-2

Publisher's Cataloging-in-Publication data

Names:
Title:
Description: .
Identifiers: ISBN | LCCN
Subjects:

Printed in the United States of America 2021 — 1st ed

TABLE OF CONTENTS

INTRODUCTION

INTRODUCTION

Almost all Christians have much confusion about God's goodness and how that goodness relates to their personal experience of adversity (things not going well in their life). They view life through their difficult experiences, and thus, their real (true in their soul) perspective is that God is really not that good. This is based on faulty understanding of God and our life here in this world. They have been taught:

1. God is in control of everything.

2. Thus, God is in control of my life.

3. Which means, everything that happens to me is God's will. Since He is in control, whatever happens to me must be His will.

4. Lots of very difficult things have happened to me, are happening to me, and it looks like it's not getting better; or when things do get better, another difficult thing happens right behind it. This is certainly not the wonderful life that I had planned out or thought was going to happen, especially being a believer and a child of God.

5. Thus, it appears that others have God's favor and blessing that is spoken of in Scripture, but not me.

6. The only conclusion that can be drawn (not said in the intellect or to others, since that is not what Christians are supposed to say) is that God just is not that good, or at least not to me. Why does all this bad stuff happen in the world, and especially to me, if He is in control? No matter how much I try to say, "This must be God's will for my own good, and I am supposed to live with it." We call this Christian fatalism; it is something my heart just cannot accept (and rightly so).

7. So, underneath it all, there is a deep disappointment with God, a degree of anger and resignation. This, then, results in me not having an intimate relationship with God through abiding in the Word, through prayer, and in the Spirit. Why bother? It does not seem to matter. Further, the best thing I can do is work really hard with my best thinking to try to overcome my adversities

> "The very conclusions we reach and the acceptance of the adversity as normal actually serves to perpetuate our adversity."

and hope that God does some things to help me. Though, if things do seem to get better, I do not expect this to last. I will pray, put on the smiling Christian face and say things are fine, but I do not really expect answers to prayers and will likely continue to have difficulty.

This has been a strategic trick of the enemy. The very conclusions we reach and the acceptance of the adversity as normal actually serves to perpetuate our adversity. We do know there is an enemy, but since God is in control and has gained victory over principalities and powers at the cross, does He not have the ability to keep the enemy away from my life? Is there any hope at all, or are we just to accept this very difficult life as normal? Should we accept that we are sinners and are going to fail, that bad things happen, and that God uses it all to teach us things? Or, do we see God as not very good, someone who seems cruel and unwilling to take better care of His children? Are we just supposed to put up with adversity as a way of life and as Christians are relegated to this life, and this is all part of God's will? Are adversity and suffering just a way that God is teaching us things, particularly to be sanctified, meaning the harder the lesson the more sanctified I will become? This, to us, seems long and hard, especially if we aren't sure we are learning a lesson (especially since we tend to repeat it).

This course will take us through the Word to help us see the truth that God is absolutely good! He has wonderful plans for us. We will experience adversity. Some is normal, as the Bible tells us that in this world, we will have trouble. Some is from God, but much is not. The good news is that there are remedies for all of them; and we need to learn exactly what it is, what are the sources and causes, and how we are to overcome adversity in our lives.

LESSON 1:
UNDERSTANDING A PLANNED LIFE AND THE EFFECTS OF THE FALL

Adversity did not just come upon mankind as part of God's original plan. Rather, it came upon us as a result of the *Fall of Adam and Eve*, who exercised their self-will, disobeyed God's instruction to not eat of the tree of the Knowledge of Good and Evil, and died as God had warned (meaning the Holy Spirit departed from their nature). As a result, Satan gained authority and power over this Earth; and this power is pure destruction, designed to steal, kill, and destroy. Adversity came about because of man's selfishness and the opposing power of Satan that is now operating where things are difficult, painful, frustrating, hard, annoying, oppressive, confusing, etc. Adversity now is normal and ever present.

REVIEW: GOD'S ORIGINAL PLAN FOR MANKIND

God's original plan for mankind is recorded in Genesis 1 and 2, which were written before the Fall. He set forth the exceptional life that Adam and Eve enjoyed before the Fall, which was His original plan. In chapters 2 and 3, it is revealed what life with Him looks like after the Fall. This exceptional life included these seven exceptional gifts:

1. Exceptional Authority: Victory and Power to Loose and Bind

Authority is defined in the Scriptures as dominion and power manifested in many different ways:

- Splendor, majesty, beauty, vigor, glory
- In-charge, control, have jurisdiction, power to influence, cause to become
- Great, much; many; enlarged, exceedingly abundant
- Power (physical and spiritual) of doing the supernatural
- Right to govern, rule, command (possessing authority)
- Mighty work, strength, miracle
- Performing miracles
- Excellence

> "All authority emanates from Him, as He is and has the ultimate authority, which is the ability to create material from the spiritual."

> **Read Genesis 1:1–3:**
> The Creation of the World
> **1** In the beginning, God created the heavens and the earth. ² The earth was without form and void, and darkness was over the face of the deep. And the Spirit of God was hovering over the face of the waters.
> ³ And God said, "Let there be light," and there was light.

First, we must understand the very nature of God's creation: He "spoke" it into existence from nothing (ex-nihilo). God is Spirit: invisible, omniscient, omnipresent, omnipotent. All authority emanates from Him, as He is and has the ultimate authority, which is the ability to create material from the spiritual. His creation is from His spoken Word.

> **Read John 1:1–3:**
> The Word Became Flesh: **1** In the beginning was the Word, and the Word was with God, and the Word was God. ² He was in the beginning with God. ³ All things were made through him, and without him was not any thing made that was made.

The spiritual trumps the material and is superior to the material; thus, the material is subordinate to the spiritual and under its authority. This is key for us to understand, as it explains why nothing is too difficult for Him; and why His power can change our circumstances, especially the adversity against us.

> **Read Genesis 1:26–27:**
> ²⁶ Then God said, "Let us make man[a] in our image, after our likeness. And let them have dominion over the fish of the sea and over the birds of the heavens and over the livestock and over all the earth and over every creeping thing that creeps on the earth."
>
> ²⁷ So God created man in his own image,
>   in the image of God he created him;
>   male and female he created them.

God created man in "Our" image. Who is "Our?" It is the Trinity—the Father, Son, and Holy Spirit are the triune God. One God, yet each distinct, and all the nature and characteristics of God are resident in all three. This includes authority. God originally gave this authority (dominion) over mankind to rule the Earth and be co-creators with Him in perfect communion with Him as created beings—with body (material), soul (seat of our personality, intellect, emotion, and will), and Spirit (His Spirit in us as ruler and leader of our lives). We were to live out this authority on Earth as we walked with Him and subdued the earth under the authority given us.

2. Exceptional Provision:

Read Genesis 1:28–30:

28 And God blessed them. And God said to them, "Be fruitful and multiply and fill the earth and subdue it, and have dominion over the fish of the sea and over the birds of the heavens and over every living thing that moves on the earth." 29 And God said, "Behold, I have given you every plant yielding seed that is on the face of all the earth, and every tree with seed in its fruit. You shall have them for food. 30 And to every beast of the earth and to every bird of the heavens and to everything that creeps on the earth, everything that has the breath of life, I have given every green plant for food." And it was so.

God provided all that was needed to live and enjoy the fullness of His creation—all the plants, animals, and materials (organic and inorganic) were created so that we lacked nothing. It was all for our benefit to use, to build, and to make new things as we so were led through being co-creator with Him—and all this was subordinate to the spiritual. The word give means that He grants us, gives over to us, and delivers up to us all this exceptional provision. We would never be short of anything needed and were to enjoy abundance, so we would not have to be concerned about living conditions or making things work in this material world.

3. Exceptional Work:

Read Genesis 2:15:

[15] The Lord God took the man and put him in the garden of Eden to work it and keep it.

God gave to man and woman the assignment of "work," occupation and labor that served the purposes of God. They were to keep and care for this world through daily, meaningful occupation, which is simply defined as what we "do" every day to occupy our time in tasks for the benefit of progress and co-creating with God. Thus, this is not about earning income, but rather working at something we truly enjoy. So, a housewife who thoroughly enjoys taking care of children and the duties of being a wife is in an exceptional "occupation." We must understand that this is a part of God's nature that was given to mankind before the Fall; work is good and to be fulfilled by all of us. It brings much to us in the form of satisfaction, fulfillment, accomplishment, community with others, joy, and fun.

4. Exceptional Marriage and Relationship:

Read Genesis 2:18–25:

[18] Then the Lord God said, "It is not good that the man should be alone; I will make him a helper fit for[a] him." [19] Now out of the ground the Lord God had formed[b] every beast of the field and every bird of the heavens and brought them to the man to see what he would call them. And whatever the man called every living creature, that was its name. [20] The man gave names to all livestock and to the birds of the heavens and to every beast of the field. But for Adam[c] there was not found a helper fit for him. [21] So the Lord God caused a deep sleep to fall upon the man, and while he slept took one of his ribs and closed up its place with flesh. [22] And the rib that the Lord God had taken from the man he made[d] into a woman and brought her to the man. [23] Then the man said,

---

> "This at last is bone of my bones
>   and flesh of my flesh;
> she shall be called Woman,
>   because she was taken out of Man."[e]
> 24 Therefore a man shall leave his father and his mother and hold fast to his wife, and they shall become one flesh. 25 And the man and his wife were both naked and were not ashamed.

God said it is not good that man be alone, so He created "Wo-man" out of man, to be a helpmate, his counterpart in intimate relationship while living here on Earth. He said the two are to leave their father and mother. It is interesting that Adam and Eve had no mother and father. So, of what was He speaking? He was saying that all who were to come thereafter were to leave their upbringing behind and forge a new way together as a couple—to come together as one—living in unity and agreement. They were to live this way only with each other, as together they walked in the Spirit in complete unity with God, with the authority and dominion given to them as co-creators over Earth. As we live in unity in our exceptional marriage, it will be a place of blessing.

> **Read Psalm 133:**
>
> When Brothers Dwell in Unity
> A Song of Ascents. Of David.
> **133** Behold, how good and pleasant it is
>   when brothers dwell in unity![a]
> 2 It is like the precious oil on the head,
>   running down on the beard,
> on the beard of Aaron,
>   running down on the collar of his robes!
> 3 It is like the dew of Hermon,
>   which falls on the mountains of Zion!
> For there the Lord has commanded the blessing,
>   life forevermore.

God states that it is good (most wonderful and favorable) and pleasant (delightful, lovely, fantastic) to dwell (live) in unity (united-ness, agreement, oneness). There He commands (orders, brings about with certainty) blessings—gifts of favor, prosperity, good things. So, through living in an exceptional marriage in unity, He promises His favor in life. Why would we not live there?

Note: Think about God's original plan for mankind: Since we are physical, and thus, need to sleep for rest and recuperation, we were to get up to go to work and enjoy our exceptional occupation during the day; then, after work we were to go home and enjoy our exceptional marriage and family life.

Read Ecclesiastes 5:18–20; 9:9–10:

[18] Behold, what I have seen to be good and fitting is to eat and drink and find enjoyment[a] in all the toil with which one toils under the sun the few days of his life that God has given him, for this is his lot. [19] Everyone also to whom God has given wealth and possessions and power to enjoy them, and to accept his lot and rejoice in his toil—this is the gift of God. [20] For he will not much remember the days of his life because God keeps him occupied with joy in his heart.

[9] Enjoy life with the wife whom you love, all the days of your vain[a] life that he has given you under the sun, because that is your portion in life and in your toil at which you toil under the sun. [10] Whatever your hand finds to do, do it with your might,[b] for there is no work or thought or knowledge or wisdom in Sheol, to which you are going.

God tells us there is nothing more important than enjoying our work and our marriage and family. It is to be the primary reason to rejoice and experience life to the full.

5. Exceptional Identity:

Read Genesis 1:26; 1:31:

26 Then God said, "Let us make man[a] in our image, after our likeness. And let them have dominion over the fish of the sea and over the birds of the heavens and over the livestock and over all the earth and over every creeping thing that creeps on the earth."

31 And God saw everything that he had made, and behold, it was very good. And there was evening and there was morning, the sixth day.

Adam and Eve understood that they were made in the likeness of God and were the children of the Most High God. They embraced their identity and lived fully in the bounty of the exceptional life provided by God. They did not reject it, diminish it, nor compromise on it. They lived like children of the King because they were! They were God's, and they knew it. This is reiterated in Song of Solomon 6:3: "I am my beloved's, and My beloved is mine." We are His loved ones, special and privileged to be His children.

6. Exceptional Health and Healing:

Read Genesis: 1:26–2:25:

26 Then God said, "Let us make man[a] in our image, after our likeness. And let them have dominion over the fish of the sea and over the birds of the heavens and over the livestock and over all the earth and over every creeping thing that creeps on the earth."

27 So God created man in his own image,
     in the image of God he created him;
        male and female he created them.

28 And God blessed them. And God said to them, "Be fruitful and multiply and fill the earth and subdue it, and have dominion over the fish of the sea and over the birds of the heavens and over every living thing that moves on the

---

earth." 29 And God said, "Behold, I have given you every plant yielding seed that is on the face of all the earth, and every tree with seed in its fruit. You shall have them for food. 30 And to every beast of the earth and to every bird of the heavens and to everything that creeps on the earth, everything that has the breath of life, I have given every green plant for food." And it was so. 31 And God saw everything that he had made, and behold, it was very good. And there was evening and there was morning, the sixth day.

The Seventh Day, God Rests

2 Thus the heavens and the earth were finished, and all the host of them. 2 And on the seventh day God finished his work that he had done, and he rested on the seventh day from all his work that he had done. 3 So God blessed the seventh day and made it holy, because on it God rested from all his work that he had done in creation.

The Creation of Man and Woman

4 These are the generations
of the heavens and the earth when they were created,
in the day that the Lord God made the earth and the heavens.

5 When no bush of the field[b] was yet in the land[c] and no small plant of the field had yet sprung up—for the Lord God had not caused it to rain on the land, and there was no man to work the ground, 6 and a mist[d] was going up from the land and was watering the whole face of the ground— 7 then the Lord God formed the man of dust from the ground and breathed into his nostrils the breath of life, and the man became a living creature. 8 And the Lord God planted a garden in Eden, in the east, and there he put the man whom he had formed. 9 And out of the ground the Lord God made to spring up every tree that is pleasant to the sight and good for food. The tree of life was in the midst of the garden, and the tree of the knowledge of good and evil.

10 A river flowed out of Eden to water the garden, and there it divided and became four rivers. 11 The name of the first is the Pishon. It is the one that flowed around the whole land of Havilah, where there is gold. 12 And the gold of that land is good; bdellium and onyx stone are there. 13 The name of the second river is the Gihon. It is the one that flowed around the whole land of Cush. 14 And the name of the third river is the Tigris, which flows east of Assyria. And the fourth river is the Euphrates.

> [15] The Lord God took the man and put him in the garden of Eden to work it and keep it. [16] And the Lord God commanded the man, saying, "You may surely eat of every tree of the garden, [17] but of the tree of the knowledge of good and evil you shall not eat, for in the day that you eat[e] of it you shall surely die." [18] Then the Lord God said, "It is not good that the man should be alone; I will make him a helper fit for[f] him." [19] Now out of the ground the Lord God had formed[g] every beast of the field and every bird of the heavens and brought them to the man to see what he would call them. And whatever the man called every living creature, that was its name. [20] The man gave names to all livestock and to the birds of the heavens and to every beast of the field. But for Adam[h] there was not found a helper fit for him. [21] So the Lord God caused a deep sleep to fall upon the man, and while he slept took one of his ribs and closed up its place with flesh. [22] And the rib that the Lord God had taken from the man he made[i] into a woman and brought her to the man. [23] Then the man said,
>
> "This at last is bone of my bones
>   and flesh of my flesh;
> she shall be called Woman,
>   because she was taken out of Man."[j]
>
> [24] Therefore a man shall leave his father and his mother and hold fast to his wife, and they shall become one flesh. [25] And the man and his wife were both naked and were not ashamed.

There was no sickness or illness in the Garden. God's exceptional life included health and healing. They lived in perfect health and enjoyed the beauty of not being concerned about physical issues.

7. Exceptional Communion with Him:

In Genesis 1:26–2:25 (above), since Adam and Eve had body, soul, and Spirit, they had exceptional communion with God. They had regular communications, heard clearly what He had to say, could dialogue with Him at any time, and enjoyed their designed intimacy with Him all the time. They were His children, who lived in the beauty of a special relationship with the Almighty God, the creator of the universe, and had the confidence of knowing they were living in the exceptional life provided for and given by God.

This is expressed further in John 10:3–5; 27–30:

3 To him the gatekeeper opens. The sheep hear his voice, and he calls his own sheep by name and leads them out. 4 When he has brought out all his own, he goes before them, and the sheep follow him, for they know his voice. 5 A stranger they will not follow, but they will flee from him, for they do not know the voice of strangers."

27 My sheep hear my voice, and I know them, and they follow me. 28 I give them eternal life, and they will never perish, and no one will snatch them out of my hand. 29 My Father, who has given them to me,[a] is greater than all, and no one is able to snatch them out of the Father's hand. 30 I and the Father are one."

He is our Shepherd and knows us intimately, and we hear Him (attend to, consider what is or has been said; to understand, perceive the sense of what is said; to hear something; to perceive by the ear what is announced in one's presence), know Him (to see; to perceive with the eyes; to perceive by any of the senses; to perceive, notice, discern, discover) and follow Him (willingly go with Him where He leads us).

He also describes this in John 15:1–8:

I Am the True Vine

15 "I am the true vine, and my Father is the vinedresser. 2 Every branch in me that does not bear fruit he takes away, and every branch that does bear fruit he prunes, that it may bear more fruit. 3 Already you are clean because of the word that I have spoken to you. 4 Abide in me, and I in you. As the branch cannot bear fruit by itself, unless it abides in the vine, neither can you, unless you abide in me. 5 I am the vine; you are the branches. Whoever abides in me and I in him, he it is that bears much fruit, for apart from me you can do nothing. 6 If anyone does not abide in me he is thrown away like a branch and withers; and the branches are gathered, thrown into the fire, and burned. 7 If you abide in me, and my words abide in you, ask whatever you wish, and it will be done for you. 8 By this my Father is glorified, that you bear much fruit and so prove to be my disciples.

We are intimately connected to Him as the Branch to the Vine, with the Vinedresser (The Father) directing our lives through making our decisions. We remain in Him, and as a result, we bear fruit, more fruit, and much fruit. We glorify Him, as we abide in Him through our intimate relationship. Adam and Eve fully understood, "Apart from Him, we can do nothing." Why? Because of exceptional communion. How special is that!

Summary: In Genesis 1:31 it states: "Then God saw everything (all these exceptional characteristics of life with Him) that He had made, and indeed it was very good. So, the evening and the morning were the sixth day. The Earth was perfect. It had no destructive forces, no sin, no pain, no sickness, and no adversity. All was good—exceptionally and abundantly good! This Hebrew word is a very strong definition of what "good" means: pleasant, agreeable (to the senses); pleasant (to the higher nature), excellent, rich, valuable in estimation: glad, happy, prosperous. These seven exceptional qualities of God's creation before the Fall were amazingly, extraordinarily, supernaturally good. This was God's original plan—nothing but spectacular with no adversity—life abundant and life eternal. We must understand this as we look at the current state of the world with its common and normal adversity.

A PROBLEM: THE FALL

This wonderful life ended. In Genesis 3:1–13, we see what happened.

The Fall

3 Now the serpent was more crafty than any other beast of the field that the Lord God had made.

He said to the woman, "Did God actually say, 'You[a] shall not eat of any tree in the garden'?" 2 And the woman said to the serpent, "We may eat of the fruit of the trees in the garden, 3 but God said, 'You shall not eat of the fruit of the tree that is in the midst of the garden, neither shall you touch it, lest you die.'" 4 But the serpent said to the woman, "You will not surely die. 5 For God knows that when you eat of it your eyes will be opened, and you will be like God, knowing good and evil." 6 So when the woman saw that the tree was good for food, and that it was a delight to the eyes, and that the tree was to be desired to make one wise,[b] she took of its fruit and ate, and she also gave some to her husband who was with her, and he ate. 7 Then the eyes of both were opened, and they knew that they were naked. And they sewed fig leaves together and made themselves loincloths.

> [8] And they heard the sound of the Lord God walking in the garden in the cool[c] of the day, and the man and his wife hid themselves from the presence of the Lord God among the trees of the garden. [9] But the Lord God called to the man and said to him, "Where are you?"[d] [10] And he said, "I heard the sound of you in the garden, and I was afraid, because I was naked, and I hid myself." [11] He said, "Who told you that you were naked? Have you eaten of the tree of which I commanded you not to eat?" [12] The man said, "The woman whom you gave to be with me, she gave me fruit of the tree, and I ate." [13] Then the Lord God said to the woman, "What is this that you have done?" The woman said, "The serpent deceived me, and I ate."

Satan had already been booted out of heaven. As Lucifer (an angel of light), he was number two in heaven with all the wonder and beauty of heaven; but decided with his free will to not choose God. God's creation of his higher beings— angels and man—include free will. True love is based upon free will—the ability to choose God or not.

> **Read Isaiah 14:12–21:**
>
> [12] "How you are fallen from heaven,
>   O Day Star, son of Dawn!
> How you are cut down to the ground,
>   you who laid the nations low!
> [13] You said in your heart,
>   'I will ascend to heaven;
> above the stars of God
>   I will set my throne on high;
> I will sit on the mount of assembly
>   in the far reaches of the north;[a]
> [14] I will ascend above the heights of the clouds;
>   I will make myself like the Most High.'
> [15] But you are brought down to Sheol,
>   to the far reaches of the pit.
> [16] Those who see you will stare at you
>   and ponder over you:
> 'Is this the man who made the earth tremble,
>   who shook kingdoms,

> ¹⁷ who made the world like a desert
> and overthrew its cities,
> who did not let his prisoners go home?'
> ¹⁸ All the kings of the nations lie in glory,
> each in his own tomb;^[b]
> ¹⁹ but you are cast out, away from your grave,
> like a loathed branch,
> clothed with the slain, those pierced by the sword,
> who go down to the stones of the pit,
> like a dead body trampled underfoot.
> ²⁰ You will not be joined with them in burial,
> because you have destroyed your land,
> you have slain your people.
> "May the offspring of evildoers
> nevermore be named!
> ²¹ Prepare slaughter for his sons
> because of the guilt of their fathers,
> lest they rise and possess the earth,
> and fill the face of the world with cities."

In these verses we read that Lucifer wanted to be like God, so he made a move to take over. Not having the power of God (we must remember that Satan is not God—not omniscient, omnipresent, omnipotent—but a created being with limitations), he did not win this challenge to God (through this free will) and was consequently cast out of heaven. In addition, all the angels in heaven were given the opportunity to exercise their free will and were offered by God whom they wanted to follow. Two thirds of the angels chose to stay with and follow God (continuing to function as angelic heavenly hosts) and one third chose to leave and follow Satan (Rev. 12: 4). So, Satan and now his demons (fallen angels) had access to Earth and to Adam and Eve, but he had no authority to bring his destruction. So, what he had to do was appeal to Adam and Eve to exercise their free will and disobey God, so that Satan could receive the authority given to Adam and Eve (in Genesis 1:26 where this authority was given to mankind), and thereby, alter the nature of Earth to be dominated by Satan's nature of destruction. Satan appealed to Eve, and thus, to Adam who was right there with her to choose to eat of the forbidden tree (the tree of the Knowledge of Good and Evil in the middle of the garden). This tree was designated by God so that there was a real choice of exercising their free will, which included the free will to either choose God or not, as had Lucifer and the demonic angels. They had been warned by God that if they ate of this tree, they would surely die. Lucifer appealed to them that God surely did not say, "You would die," and then asked if they wanted to be like God.

As is true with our free will today, the real mistake that Adam and Eve made at this point was wondering about what God really did say, and exactly what it meant. Also, they did not go back to God with their open, perfect, and exceptional communion and ask God again to speak on this. They just drew their own conclusions, based upon the temptation of what they heard from Satan. As a result, they ate of the forbidden tree. At that moment they did die, as spoken by God. What actually died? Man and woman were created as body (real material), soul (the seat of intellect, personality, emotion, and will) and spirit (God's Holy Spirit). Animals are just body and soul and driven by instincts (self- preservation). So, at the Fall, the spirit of man and woman died. The Holy Spirit had to vacate. They became a very sophisticated, intellectually superior animal now, driven by instinct and self-centeredness. Their nature changed. It became a sin nature devoid of the Spirit of God and no longer holy. This impeded their ability to have direct relationship with God, because He is holy and requires perfection. Thus, the nature of the world changed. It went from the beauty, perfection, and all the exceptional goodness of God and His original creation to the nature of Satan.

> **Read John 10:10:**
>
> [10] The thief comes only to steal and kill and destroy. I came that they may have life and have it abundantly.

This verse tells us that Satan seeks to steal, kill, and destroy. It must be noted that the only remedy is to be "born again," to have the Spirit re-enter our nature and give us the ability to receive Christ's life in us. But at the Fall, everything on Earth (both animate and inanimate) went to and is still operating in destruction, which is called entropy. This includes all things, like steel bridges that collapse in Minneapolis, like the coliseum in Rome, etc. So, everything left alone will go to destruction, and this destructive world is being led by those in power who are fallen, sinful people who operate purely selfishly. It should not surprise us, then, that the world is literally going to "hell in a hand basket" and getting more and more wicked, full of the values of anti-God. When Adam and Eve exercised their free will and disobeyed God's will, they thwarted the original plan of exceptional life in an exceptional creation and handed over the authority and sinful nature of man and the world destruction to Satan. The world is now a place of great trouble, great adversity, and great difficulty. This has become normal and is getting even more so.

The enemy's world in which we live is shown in John 10:10, which reveals the essence of the enemy. He aims to steal (take away by theft, i.e., take away by stealth); kill (put to death good things); and destroy (to put out of the way entirely, abolish, put an end to ruin, render useless). It is relentless and never ending. There is no breather. Our world is the world of the enemy, so naturally, it is a place where things oppose us and where things are not intended to go well for us. This is so that we do not seek God and learn to abide and remain in Him, but to rather blame God for these awful things that happen to us.

---

1.   Luke 4:5–8:

[5] And the devil took him up and showed him all the kingdoms of the world in a moment of time, [6] and said to him, "To you I will give all this authority and their glory, for it has been delivered to me, and I give it to whom I will. [7] If you, then, will worship me, it will all be yours." [8] And Jesus answered him, "It is written,

"'You shall worship the Lord your God,

    and him only shall you serve.'"

Satan tempts Christ by offering the kingdoms of the world to Him. He can accept this offer and then take back the authority without having to go to the cross. The intent is for Christ to just subordinate Himself to Satan. This was a real temptation, which meant that Satan actually had the ability to deliver the kingdom of the world (which was now his since it was given to him by Adam and Eve). The Greek word, "kingdom" here means power, kingship, dominion, rule, the right or authority to rule over a kingdom. "Power" is another word for authority and dominion. If it was not real, Christ would have dismissed it knowing that it was not Satan's to give, so nothing real was being offered. Rather, Christ said, "Yes, you do have this authority now," but He still chooses not to take a shortcut but only worship and follow the Father. His will was to choose God.

Note a very profound truth: Adam and Eve exercised self-will and fell into sin. The only way to restore this nature of sin now within all mankind born into the world from Adam and Eve was for God Himself (Christ) to exercise His self-will and not succumb to these temptations at the beginning of His ministry on Earth. He then needed to exercise His self-will in Gethsemane on His way to the cross at the end of His ministry, so that based upon His free will, it was purely His choice, as read in John 10:17–18:

> ¹⁷ For this reason the Father loves me, because I lay down my life that I may take it up again. ¹⁸ No one takes it from me, but I lay it down of my own accord. I have authority to lay it down, and I have authority to take it up again. This charge I have received from my Father."

He marched to the cross where the sin was placed upon Him and satisfied the Father's requirement of perfection (propitiation/sacrifice). He obtained back the authority for man to once again be "born again" through belief. This enabled us to have the Holy Spirit restored in our nature. Christ did acknowledge that Satan had the authority of worldly kingdoms operating on earth and that the nature of his kingdoms was destruction: to steal, kill, and destroy.

> **2. 1 John 5:18–20:**
>
> ¹⁸ We know that everyone who has been born of God does not keep on sinning, but he who was born of God protects him, and the evil one does not touch him. ¹⁹ We know that we are from God, and the whole world lies in the power of the evil one.
>
> ²⁰ And we know that the Son of God has come and has given us understanding, so that we may know him who is true; and we are in him who is true, in his Son Jesus Christ. He is the true God and eternal life.

John wrote 60 years after the resurrection that Satan still had control over this world. Though Christ has taken back the authority, His authority operates in His Kingdom, which now is available to us to live in; but we also live in the natural world that is still under the authority of Satan (which is what we would call enemy territory). The Greek word here for wickedness means full of labor, annoyances, hardships, pressed and harassed, toil, full of peril, pain and trouble, evil, wicked, and bad. That pretty well describes our world. It should not surprise us that this characterizes everyday life. Though believers, we live in enemy territory and are subject to this normal wickedness. As believers we are called to live in both kingdoms—within the Kingdom of God which is righteousness, peace, and joy in the Holy Spirit—while we also traverse through enemy territory in a world under the control of the enemy. This world is still characterized by destruction: steal, kill, and destroy.

Read Romans 14:17:

¹⁷ For the kingdom of God is not a matter of eating and drinking but of righteousness and peace and joy in the Holy Spirit.

We must fully understand that though Satan has been defeated by Christ, and all authority has now been given to Christ, this is spiritual authority, which does trump temporal authority. However, this is only appropriated by believers who are walking in the Spirit in His Kingdom. We exist within these two kingdoms. The worldly kingdom is still the nature of entropy with dark principalities and powers still operating. We are not exempt from this kingdom, and adversity will still occur in our everyday lives.

The Fall happened, and man received a self-centered sin nature, with which all are born. The world went from being perfect with exceptional living to one of difficulty, adversity, and wickedness as the norm. We cannot escape it and are all subject to it.

THE FATHER HAS ANOTHER PLAN TO RESTORE THE ORIGINAL PLAN: CHRIST, OUR REDEEMER, OUR RESTORER.

Though the world has been lost to destruction under the control of the enemy, and our nature is now a sin nature dominated by self, the Father has provided another plan. He has given us a Redeemer who can bring us again back to the beautiful, restored life intended by God. Salvation and being born again is not just a ticket to heaven, but it is an invitation to a restoration of the original, exceptional life intended by God in the Garden of Eden. Christ has come to bring us this exceptional life now.

1. John 10:10:

¹⁷ For the kingdom of God is not a matter of eating and drinking but of righteousness and peace and joy in the Holy Spirit.

The words spoken by Christ here are the same words used by the Father in Genesis 1:31: This life that Christ has come to give us is the exceptional, super-abundant, good life intended in the Garden of Eden. His death and resurrection conquered death and Satan, and thus, we do not have to live under the control and influence of the destructive enemy. Rather, we can reverse the destruction and receive to the point of possessing and owning this super-abundant (exceedingly, supremely, extraordinary, more remarkable, more excellent) life. This life is the full, genuine, real, active, vigorous, fullness of life of God. This is to be lived out in this destructive world, as we live in the Kingdom of God, in the Spirit, and in Christ. It is not just for heaven but for the now. Thus, while we will have adversity since we live in enemy territory, we have this exceptional, abundant life offered to us.

---

2.   Luke 4:16–21; Isaiah 61:

Jesus Rejected at Nazareth

16 And he came to Nazareth, where he had been brought up. And as was his custom, he went to the synagogue on the Sabbath day, and he stood up to read. 17 And the scroll of the prophet Isaiah was given to him. He unrolled the scroll and found the place where it was written,

18 "The Spirit of the Lord is upon me,
    because he has anointed me
    to proclaim good news to the poor.
He has sent me to proclaim liberty to the captives
    and recovering of sight to the blind,
    to set at liberty those who are oppressed,
19 to proclaim the year of the Lord's favor."

20 And he rolled up the scroll and gave it back to the attendant and sat down. And the eyes of all in the synagogue were fixed on him. 21 And he began to say to them, "Today this Scripture has been fulfilled in your hearing."

The Year of the Lord's Favor

61 The Spirit of the Lord God is upon me,
    because the Lord has anointed me
to bring good news to the poor;[a]
    he has sent me to bind up the brokenhearted,
to proclaim liberty to the captives,
    and the opening of the prison to those who are bound;[b]
2 to proclaim the year of the Lord's favor,
    and the day of vengeance of our God;
    to comfort all who mourn;
3 to grant to those who mourn in Zion—
    to give them a beautiful headdress instead of ashes,

the oil of gladness instead of mourning,
    the garment of praise instead of a faint spirit;
that they may be called oaks of righteousness,
    the planting of the Lord, that he may be glorified.[c]
4 They shall build up the ancient ruins;
    they shall raise up the former devastations;
they shall repair the ruined cities,
    the devastations of many generations.
5 Strangers shall stand and tend your flocks;
    foreigners shall be your plowmen and vinedressers;
6 but you shall be called the priests of the Lord;
    they shall speak of you as the ministers of our God;
you shall eat the wealth of the nations,
    and in their glory you shall boast.
7 Instead of your shame there shall be a double portion;
    instead of dishonor they shall rejoice in their lot;
therefore in their land they shall possess a double portion;
    they shall have everlasting joy.
8 For I the Lord love justice;
    I hate robbery and wrong;[d]
I will faithfully give them their recompense,
    and I will make an everlasting covenant with them.
9 Their offspring shall be known among the nations,
    and their descendants in the midst of the peoples;
all who see them shall acknowledge them,
    that they are an offspring the Lord has blessed.
10 I will greatly rejoice in the Lord;
    my soul shall exult in my God,
for he has clothed me with the garments of salvation;
    he has covered me with the robe of righteousness,
as a bridegroom decks himself like a priest with a beautiful headdress,
    and as a bride adorns herself with her jewels.
11 For as the earth brings forth its sprouts,
    and as a garden causes what is sown in it to sprout up,
so the Lord God will cause righteousness and praise
    to sprout up before all the nations.

LESSON 1:
UNDERSTANDING A PLANNED LIFE AND THE EFFECTS OF THE FALL

Luke 4 describes the first public statement of Christ about His ministry. He goes to the synagogue in Nazareth, which He had been to many times since He lived there, and is handed the Scroll of Isaiah 61 to read. He reads it and states publicly (after sitting down to make an emphatic point) that Isaiah 61 has been fulfilled in Him, and He has come to bring this redemptive, beautiful life to us now and not just a ticket to heaven. This beautiful life includes healing up our wounds (to bind up, repair). We are all wounded and have patterns in our lives that are destructive and cause us difficulty. Christ promises to heal us so that these wounds are fully restored to health, and thus, no longer cause us difficulty or lead us to our poor responses to things in life. Instead, they give us liberty (free-flowing freedom) and free us up from being captive. All of us are captive to certain patterns and ways of how we look at and respond to life. We can be living in un-forgiveness, full of anger, always frustrated, responding in fear, worry, and anxiety, etc., and no matter how much we try, we cannot seem to live in freedom, and thus, we remain in our captivity. Christ promises us that He will lead us to freedom and release us from our patterns of captivity so that our life is full of joy and wonder. Christ gives us comfort (brings compassion, console, hope) when we are downtrodden, burdened, grieving, and disappointed, because the situations in our lives are not working well or not what we thought they would be. We have a tendency to go to resignation and accept that this life is troublesome, is never going to be great (perhaps once in a while but certainly not as the norm), and something we just have to put up with it. Christ promises that He will give us comfort and show us how wonderful life can be as we walk with Him.

He also promises that He can make beauty (ornaments, value) from ashes. Throughout our life, we often ruin or have ruined things that literally are ashes (of no value and no hope of amounting to anything). Christ has such amazing supernatural power that He can bring worthless, dead things back to life, back to value, and back to such beauty that it is exceptional (i.e., the original exceptional life of Genesis). He can deliver joy and praise from things that have not gone well and are heavy and weighing on us. Instead of going to worry, fear, and anxiety, He causes us to experience true joy and praise to the extent that we are thrilled at the life He has brought and the hope of the promises ahead, even if we are currently experiencing difficulty.

Further, He promises to build up and repair from our ruins (construct, rebuild, re-establish to original, make new again). Isn't this wonderful? What we have ruined through our sin and terrible choices can all be restored to God's original plan, and it matters not how much it is ruined. This is the Good News. He can redeem and restore anything! He can take what has been ruined by the enemy (stolen, killed, and destroyed) or by us through not following Him, and He can make it beautiful, restored, or rebuilt. This sums up the wonderful ministry of Christ today. It's not just a ticket to heaven, but it has come to give us the abundant, exceptional life now that He has uniquely planned for us. Remember, He is not a respecter of persons, with some being lucky and others not. He has come and offers exceptional life to all who are His children.

The people of the world now have a clear choice. We can continue to live as self-centered people in a fallen world that is self-destructing, or we can live as a child of God who is redeemed. Then the children of God have two choices to make: (1) to live in His kingdom through abiding in Him ("Apart from Him we can do nothing" – John 15:5), walking in the Spirit, and thus, experiencing the restoration of the exceptional life ("I have come to give you life and give it super abundantly" – John 10:10); or (2) live a carnal life in the flesh (remain self-centered) and again put to death the Spirit (still resident in us, but operating as if not there), be at enmity against God's will (live outside His Kingdom life), and not able to please Him (Romans 8:5–8). As we will see in Section 2, by living in the Kingdom and abiding and walking in the Spirit, we cannot avoid all adversity. There are certain adversities that are brought purposely by God to cause us to repent and turn away from our carnal living as a believer, so these adversities will be experienced, though they need not be.

For the unbeliever there is a deepening sense of adversity that characterizes their life on a global and national level, as well as on a personal level. There is judgment against mankind on a global, national, local, and personal level, because the truth stands, regardless of whether we seek it or understand it; and there really is no excuse, since there is built within us a sense that there is something greater than us. There are plenty of physical indicators available to all who can see that there is something greater than us. Romans 1:18 and 2:16 explain this in great detail. The wrath (judgment of God) is revealed against all ungodliness, for God has revealed Himself to all, and thus, none are without excuse. They are living futile lives and are foolishly thinking they are wise having exchanged the glory of the incorruptible God for the corruptible idols of man. Because of this, God gives them over to their sad, adversity-filled lives and their evil passions (like homosexuality, greed, adultery, strife, deceit, etc.) that only promote more adversity. Those who are self-seeking and do not seek nor follow the truth, but rather pursue unrighteousness which they have believed to be righteous, will experience indignation, wrath, tribulation, and anguish. In other words, they receive major adversity as normal. If we step from our own time back in history and look at all of history visiting each era and observing, we would basically see awful, difficult things and great adversity all over the place. Regardless of our station in life, none of us would want to go back to another time if we really knew what it was like. We Americans have been blessed, because we were a nation under God and received blessings of prosperity, standard of living, freedom, avoidance of war on our soil (except civil war between ourselves), and the expectation and hope that things would always get better. Thus, our level of general adversity (see description in Chapter 4) has been relatively protected and contained, because we were a nation under God.

Today, I believe that is not so, and we are suffering the consequences of Romans 1 and 2 as a nation. God is giving over our nation to its uncleanness and vile passions, withdrawing His protection over adversity and actually bringing about His promised indignation, wrath, tribulation, and anguish. It is going to get worse, and those of us who are still living in the Kingdom of God are not exempt from this global and national scale of adversity, which characterizes most of history on earth. Our lives are going to become more difficult, frustrating, and painful, not because our government and rulers cannot quite get it right regardless of political persuasion, but because we are dealing in spiritual things and live outside of God's protection, it will typically be full of adversity. This should not surprise us, nor should we think that we are exempt.

SUMMARY of LESSON 1:

- God originally planned an exceptional life for His creation, mankind:

  - Exceptional Authority
  - Exceptional Provision
  - Exceptional Work
  - Exceptional Marriage
  - Exceptional Identity
  - Exceptional Health and Healing
  - Exceptional Communion with God

Adam and Eve fully enjoyed this life in the Garden of Eden. It was theirs to enjoy, and it truly was exceptional. This life is a picture for us to see as His original plan; a plan though lost through the Fall of man, is still available to us today.

- Satan came and tempted Adam and Eve by appealing to them to exercise their self-will by disobeying God and His instruction to not eat of the tree of the Knowledge of Good and Evil; and that if they did, they would surely die. They did go to "self" and ate of the tree, and surely did die. They lost the Spirit that was resident in them. They handed over to Satan the authority of the Earth that had been given to them by God; and as a result, Satan gained control over the world with an operation of destruction—steal, kill, and destroy—which is entropy, where everything is going to decay, and finally, destruction. So, with sinful, selfish mankind living on Earth and operating as a sophisticated animal with self-centered decisions and the Earth becoming a place of destruction, our life is going to experience trouble, tribulation, difficulty, annoyance, hardship, oppression, bad things happening, adversity. It is now normal, and until Christ returns, is also irreversible. We live in enemy territory and cannot escape the difficult place we live in.

- God provided another way. He brought His new Kingdom where He can restore His original plan—the exceptional life—to those who believe and walk in what He has provided. Through Christ's redemptive work at the cross, where He took the penalty for the deserved punishment for sin, we were given back the authority that was lost by mankind to Satan. Those who believe (and are born again and have the Spirit reenter their life) now have the opportunity to overcome the destructive world we live in and have Christ restore to us His original plan of the exceptional, abundant life. Thus, we live in two kingdoms—the Kingdom of God, which is superior in power and might; and the kingdom of Earth that is still controlled by Satan with the nature of destruction and entropy. As believers, we have the choice to "walk in the Spirit" and operate in His Kingdom, under His rulership, leading and guiding, and under His supernatural work in, through, and around us; or, we can live in the carnal (self) and leave the Kingdom life and be subject to the kingdom of the world and all its destruction—and will surely experience adversity. It is our choice (Deuteronomy 30:11–20): We can choose Him and walk in the Kingdom where there is life and blessing; or by not choosing Him and not walking in the Kingdom, we experience death and curses. Since we live in the two kingdoms with its exceptional life of God, in the middle of enemy territory with its destructive forces, we are to understand that adversity is always present. It should not surprise us that adversity will impact our lives, even as we are living in the Kingdom and experiencing His exceptional life for us.

The key is to understand the nature of adversity, the different causes of adversity, and then our responses to the adversity in these different scenarios.

LESSON 2:
TYPES AND CAUSES OF REAL ADVERSITY

"There are multiple causes of adversity. Our understanding of these in our specific situations is crucial to how we respond to these adversities. "

Let's look at the typical types of adversity that we face in our lives:

1. Frustration – This comes when things are not going well, things are not working, there are delays, traffic, red lights, delivery did not come on time, order that came was incorrect, things break down (particularly when needed – i.e., the air conditioner on a hot day).

    Satan wants to make frustration and move us out of the Kingdom. This causes us so to lose our peace, joy, freedom, and perhaps then moves us to selfishness where we lose protection and onto a path of his direct attack.

2. Life Difficulties – The severity of these determine our reaction to and our level of anxiety. Perhaps we have financial reversal (stock market bottoms out to a position that we were not expecting; an asset we own, like a boat, house, or rental property, has an unexpected financial loss, a renter doesn't pay for damages made to a property), a car accident (particularly if not our fault), a business issue (customer loss or major complaint, or major service issue, employee loss, complaint, or lawsuit, poor performance by employees, vendor loss, new government law or lawsuit, new costs, inability to pass on costs to customer through price increases, drop in margin, change in technology, economic model changing, cash flow issues, market changes, or you're feeling tired and weary and stuck; no margin), or working too much, or government actions that change our way of life (like COVID-19 with quarantines, economic shutdown, limited freedom to operate, wearing masks, limited social gatherings for sports, concerts, church worship, etc.).

3. Relationship Issues – If your marriage is not doing well, you are angry at each other, arguing much of the time, or have other family issues, or the kids are not doing well because they've made poor choices and are suffering with their consequences, and while you feel bad for them and are trying to help, but find you are not really helping. Or, you find that parents and siblings are operating in

dysfunctional ways and affecting your family and you; church has similar dysfunctional issues that affect you, especially if in a leadership role. Or maybe you have friends who are causing problems; or maybe you have opposition from specific individuals in business, ministry, community groups and are against you and what you believe to be the will and promises of God either directly or indirectly. And, to you, things not only lack progression, but even seem to be sliding backward.

4. Health Issues – Are you experiencing physical problems? The range of issues includes colds/flus that last awhile that are just nuisances to severe accidents to long-term disabilities to long-term, life-ending diagnoses, such as cancer. We can go from enjoying a normal physical life to all of a sudden living a life consumed by the physical condition that needs a resolution because it is limiting our ability to function normally, even temporarily as with the cold/flu. One of the enemy's techniques is to get us to accept this as "God's will" so we now spend the rest of our life or a period of our life hampered and less than best and limited in living the abundant life. God uses the physical to get our attention about something spiritual going on, since it is so critical to our well-being and we cannot ignore it.

5. Surprises – In any of the above categories and those we cannot even imagine, something can happen beyond our control, out of the blue, suddenly. It can even be global (a war starts, the stock market declines, and we lose big), a new law is passed, a new competitor enters the market (Uber into the taxi market), someone in our world decides to go after us, our company, or you personally, etc., and it changes our world as we must now focus on this new adversity.

WHAT KIND OF ADVERSITIES ARE YOU ENCOUNTERING RIGHT NOW? DESCRIBE IN DETAIL AND THE EFFECT THEY ARE HAVING AT THE MOMENT.

_____

_____

_____

_____

_____

_____

_____

_____

_____

LESSON 2:
TYPES AND CAUSES OF REAL ADVERSITY

CAUSES OF ADVERSITY

There are multiple causes of adversity. Our understanding of these in our specific situations is crucial to how we respond to these adversities. With this understanding, we shall be better equipped to live out the abundant life for which Christ came and that He promised to give us.

GENERAL ADVERSITY

What will we experience? Why?

What does Jesus tell us about what will happen to us in this world? Why? What does this mean for our everyday lives?

Read John 16:33:

[33] I have said these things to you, that in me you may have peace. In the world you will have tribulation. But take heart; I have overcome the world."

_____

_____

_____

_____

_____

Jesus makes the initial statement that in the world we are going to have trouble (He has overcome it, and we have the opportunity to have His shalom—His peace resolution). But in the world will be trouble. Is anybody exempt from this? No. We all will experience this trouble. The words here are pressure, oppression, affliction, distress. In the world, everybody is going to have this pressure, this tribulation, this distress. And so, it's general adversity for all.

It's not unique. It's not special. It affects everybody all at the same time, and you just happen to be part of the everybody. So, it's general adversity. The nature of the world is to steal, kill, and destroy anything that is good. And I am living in this world of entropy that is destruction. Everything left alone is going to destruction as self-centered people operate with destruction. Everything functioning is going to break down. Everything is going to fail. You're going to deal with self-centered people. You're going to deal with things that are coming against us in general. It's not unique to you.

Once you understand general adversity, it doesn't surprise you when it comes. And it's not personal. For example, appliances in your house break down; it happens because mechanical things in the world break down. It is not unique or personal to you. Your coffee machine breaks down. Your washer and dryer break down. Your air conditioner breaks down.

It's not unique in general, but it can be. And this is where we must have discernment. You need to consider if this could be an attack of Satan. Are you in a situation where you have this important meeting and Satan is trying to attack you and prevent this from happening? Maybe your car or some other mechanical thing is breaking down so that Satan can attempt to prevent you from attending your meeting? Is this unique to you? Yes. Nevertheless, much that happens in our everyday lives is general adversity, not unique to us because it happens to everybody, and it happens because we are just part of this destructive world that is full of adversity. Christ tells us that things will happen, and we should not be surprised by them.

Word Definitions: **peace:** shalom

trouble: pressing, pressing together, pressure, oppression, affliction, tribulation, distress, straits

courage: good cheer

overcome: conquer, to carry off the victory, come off victorious, of Christ, victorious over all His foes

---

Remember John 10:10:

[10] The thief comes only to steal and kill and destroy. I came that they may have life and have it abundantly.

This is the essence of the enemy: steal, kill, and destroy; relentless and never ending; no breather.

Word Definitions: **thief:** abuse their confidence for their own gain

steal: take away by theft, (i.e., take away by stealth)

destroy: to put out of the way entirely, abolish, put an end to, ruin, render useless

What are the normal reasons in business and life that we face problems? What does this mean to our lives?

Read Psalm 107:23–28:

23 Some went down to the sea in ships,
   doing business on the great waters;
24 they saw the deeds of the Lord,
   his wondrous works in the deep.
25 For he commanded and raised the stormy wind,
   which lifted up the waves of the sea.
26 They mounted up to heaven; they went down to the depths;
   their courage melted away in their evil plight;
27 they reeled and staggered like drunken men
   and were at their wits' end.[a]
28 Then they cried to the Lord in their trouble,
   and he delivered them from their distress.

_____

_____

_____

_____

_____

_____

Further, in business and in regular life, general adversity happens, and this is normal, albeit difficult. Storms are part of life, and we are not exempt. It happens to all and is not unique to us. Just as in this description of being at sea and a storm comes up, it is normal and going to happen. We are not to be surprised and not to think this is special to us. We need to accept these storms, these typical rough times in life as general adversity.

LESSON 2:
TYPES AND CAUSES OF REAL ADVERSITY

Word Definitions: **stagger:** quiver, totter, shake, reel, stagger, wander, move, sift, make move, wave, waver, tremble

trouble: narrow, tight, straits, distress

wit's end: end of their wisdom, skill (in war), (in administration), shrewdness, prudence

If the mountains are shaking, what does that mean for us? How should we react to this?

Read Psalm 46:1–7:

God Is Our Fortress
To the choirmaster. Of the Sons of Korah. According to Alamoth.[a] A Song.
46 God is our refuge and strength,
  a very present[b] help in trouble.
² Therefore we will not fear though the earth gives way,
  though the mountains be moved into the heart of the sea,
³ though its waters roar and foam,
  though the mountains tremble at its swelling. Selah
⁴ There is a river whose streams make glad the city of God,
  the holy habitation of the Most High.
⁵ God is in the midst of her; she shall not be moved;
  God will help her when morning dawns.
⁶ The nations rage, the kingdoms totter;
  he utters his voice, the earth melts.
⁷ The Lord of hosts is with us;
  the God of Jacob is our fortress. Selah

_____

_____

_____

_____

_____

If the mountains are shaking (a big shaking felt by many), I'm not the only one experiencing this trouble. It's probable that other people are also feeling it—unbelievers, believers, me, my family, everybody else who happens to be around those mountains. It is "global and broad" and is not just affecting me personally. We are to understand that what's going on here is bigger than us as individuals. I just happened to be where it is happening. I'm part of this life of trouble, and it is general.

Word Definitions: **trouble:** straits, distress
shake: quake
troubled: be in turmoil

What is trouble? How does it affect us, and how do we react to it?

Read Psalm 91:14–16:

[14] "Because he holds fast to me in love, I will deliver him;
 I will protect him, because he knows my name.
[15] When he calls to me, I will answer him;
 I will be with him in trouble;
 I will rescue him and honor him.
[16] With long life I will satisfy him
 and show him my salvation."

_____

_____

_____

_____

_____

The psalmist describes generic trouble when you're in a "pressing which is happening in a broader sense and not unique to you"; it's just general trouble. This means we should not be so surprised when it happens to us. It's not unique to you, it's not caused by you, and it's not directed toward you. It's not even Satan coming directly against you. You're just caught in the world at this place. And it's happening to lots of people.

Remember this interesting twist, however. Often people look at the adversity that they are experiencing as "general" when it really is that they are not living out the life of God. For example, I'm having financial difficulty, and I say it's general adversity. The truth is that this is not general adversity but because I am not tithing, which carries with it adversity because I am being disobedient (we will deal with this later). So, you might have to go deeper and not attribute all adversity as general. There indeed are times to consider this. There will be further understanding that will be critical to our processing this.

Word Definition: **trouble:** straits, distress

TEST OF FAITH

What does God say about this type of trial? What is it for? Why?

> **Read James 1:2–5:**
>
> Testing of Your Faith
> [2] Count it all joy, my brothers,[a] when you meet trials of various kinds, [3] for you know that the testing of your faith produces steadfastness. [4] And let steadfastness have its full effect, that you may be perfect and complete, lacking in nothing.
>
> [5] If any of you lacks wisdom, let him ask God, who gives generously to all without reproach, and it will be given him.

_____

_____

_____

_____

_____

This states that we are to count it all joy when we encounter a tribulation or a trial of many kinds, because this is a testing of your faith. This means this adversity (this trial, this trouble) comes from God directly. The word here means an experiment; to prove out. So, when you read it, look at it this way: count it all joy when God brings an experiment to prove out our faith. This is from Him with a single purpose: to prove out your faith.

And that's from God. This is a trial from God. This is an adversity from God purposely to test out your faith.

Word Definitions: **joy:** gladness
trials: experiment, attempt, proving
testing: the proving, tried

What is the purpose of these trials? What is God doing for us in these? Why?

Read 1 Peter 1:3–9:

Born Again to a Living Hope
[3] Blessed be the God and Father of our Lord Jesus Christ! According to his great mercy, he has caused us to be born again to a living hope through the resurrection of Jesus Christ from the dead, [4] to an inheritance that is imperishable, undefiled, and unfading, kept in heaven for you, [5] who by God's power are being guarded through faith for a salvation ready to be revealed in the last time. [6] In this you rejoice, though now for a little while, if necessary, you have been grieved by various trials, [7] so that the tested genuineness of your faith—more precious than gold that perishes though it is tested by fire—may be found to result in praise and glory and honor at the revelation of Jesus Christ. [8] Though you have not seen him, you love him. Though you do not now see him, you believe in him and rejoice with joy that is inexpressible and filled with glory, [9] obtaining the outcome of your faith, the salvation of your souls.

_____

_____

_____

_____

_____

He states here that the super abundant life is going to require faith; and it is His work, which will require the experiment of proving this faith out in you. He discusses refining; proving out that you have the real stuff. Real faith, which He is providing, which He is bringing. It's for me. He uses this testing of your response to adversity about the issue of faith to prove that you have faith. So, let's understand exactly what is faith that needs to be tested.

Word Definitions: **trials:** experiment, attempt, proving

testing: the proving, tried

more precious: more valuable

refined: to test, examine, prove, scrutinize (to see whether a thing is genuine or not), as metals, to recognize as genuine after examination, to approve, deem worthy

Faith defined:

What do these verses speak about faith? What is important to understand about the definition of faith? Why?

Read Hebrews 11:1–3:

By Faith

11 Now faith is the assurance of things hoped for, the conviction of things not seen. ² For by it the people of old received their commendation. ³ By faith we understand that the universe was created by the word of God, so that what is seen was not made out of things that are visible.

_____

_____

_____

_____

_____

Now, faith is the substance, substance of things hoped.

We understand that the world was framed or created by the Word of God so that the things that are seen were not made of things which are visible.

So, first of all, this goes back to what we've already learned as God created the world. He says in verse three, the world, the creation, which includes us, was created by Him speaking it into existence. So, the material is subordinated to the spiritual. And we know that because of what happened with Adam and Eve, when everything was together in purity (the spiritual and the physical were in unity together). So, did they have to operate by faith? No. They just operated in complete unison by sight, because it was together. There was no faith required because it was all visible.

But when they fell, what was separated? The spiritual and the physical. And now we deal with the sin nature with the physical and the spiritual being separated. In order to unify that, we must reunite the spiritual and the physical. Adversity is going to be overcome by Him reuniting the spiritual with the physical, by me conquering the physical. What is your problem? Maybe I have physical problems. My physical problem is in the natural where I live. Why do you have adversity? The physical issues are collapsing, are not working. Are there things that are not working that are causing pressure, stress, negative outcomes. My business isn't working. My ministry isn't working. My relationships aren't working. My health isn't working. There's something that is physically falling apart, and the only way He can overcome it is through spiritual restoration. He said that's why faith is required. So, He sets it up, and then he defines it. Faith is the substance, so it's real and gives us certainty. I know of things not seen. In other words, those things that haven't happened yet.

Faith, then, is seeing it before it happens. Do you believe it before it happens, even though you haven't seen it yet? This isn't how many of us operate, however. We operate by sight, and we basically attribute God's will to whatever happens, happens; whatever I see and whatever occurs, happens. And that was God's will. I will wait until after it happens.

So, there's no faith required in the belief in whatever happens, happens. Why have I decided this is the way God operates? Because my fundamental belief is that God is in control and everything that He does physically, is automatically His will. So, this adversity that happened must be His will because I operate by sight, and I don't actually consider faith at all. The only faith I have that I think is even important is that I believe God, that there is a God and that I have accepted Christ. I get to go to heaven. That's the only place faith exists. If I believe, then I get to go to heaven. The rest of it doesn't matter. Whatever happens, happens.

And since I believe that God is in control, and if God really loves me, He'll have me live a decent life. By the way, I don't live a decent life. So, my question underneath it all, which I don't tell anybody, is that I don't think that God is all that good, which is a struggle of the heart, and explains why many people do not actually read the Bible. Why should they bother reading?

Whatever happens, happens. But wait a second. Remember? Faith is a certainty of things not seen. And He just told you the definition. Could you be certain? There's only one thing you can be certain of not seeing: What He says. What he speaks. What He just told you. Faith is what He says. That's how He created the world, and that's what He can do to overcome circumstances. You must have certainty of what I speak.

That means that you get to hear His voice, to hear what He has to say, so that you will act accordingly and then you will get to a place of believing it will happen. If I said to you, "Tomorrow night all of us are going to a restaurant and I'm going to pay for your dinner at that restaurant and to be there at six o'clock," what, then, will you do at six o'clock? You will go to the restaurant. It hasn't happened yet. Why would you go there? Because I said so, and you have learned that I'm trustworthy enough to verify that I will do what I say. Here's what you won't do: call me up every 20 minutes. Are you going? Are you going? Are you going to go there? Are you going to really pay and really going to do it? Are you sure you're going to do it? You also wouldn't talk yourself out of it by thinking that I am not going to go. Or, decide that I may go, but will not pay. Or, even, you decide not to go because I likely won't show up. And you talk yourself out of it. Why? Well, there's no certainty with it. And even though I said it, which you did hear, you never went to the place of believing it, and the only way that you could act, according to what I said, is if you had certainty that what I said was accurate. You had to have certainty it would happen before it actually did. That is what you must settle.

This is faith, which is why He needs to test it. We will continue to pursue this teaching.

Word Definitions: **faith:** to be persuaded, to allow one's self to be persuaded; to be induced to

believe: to have complete confidence in a thing

substance: that which has foundation, is firm; that which has actual existence; a substance, real being – title deed, ownership

hope: expectation of good, joy

assurance/conviction: a proof, that by which a thing is proved or tested, certainty;

things: that which has been done, a deed, an accomplished fact; what is done or being accomplished

not seen: to perceive by the senses, to feel; to discover by use, to know by experience

good report: to be a witness, to bear witness, (i.e., to affirm that one has seen or heard or experienced something, or that he knows it because taught by divine)

framed: complete; to fit out, equip, put in order, arrange, adjust

Word of God: Rhema

not visible: to become evident, to be brought forth into the light, come to view, appear

What must we understand about the importance of faith? Why? What is to be our role in receiving faith?

> **Read Hebrews 11:6:**
>
> [6] And without faith it is impossible to please him, for whoever would draw near to God must believe that he exists and that he rewards those who seek him.

_____

_____

_____

_____

_____

This is a very important truth of the Christian life: We cannot live out the Christian life without faith – for without faith, it is impossible to please God. Our role is to believe that He is the great "I AM" – the I AM who can handle everything we face—every adversity we face—and that He is a rewarder of those who diligently seek Him. What's the reward? Faith itself! Since this is what is required to please Him, He says He will reward us with what is required – faith, which He will give you.

Well, that's good news. We think the burden is on us by needing to get more faith. "I have to get more faith; I have to get more faith. It's up to me. But, I can't get there. I'll never get there. I'll never please Him. So why bother?" He says: "How about if I just give it to you?" He will reveal to us how that works.

Word Definitions: **believe:** to think to be true, to be persuaded of, to credit, place confidence in the thing believed
I AM: Name of God to mean everything there is, everything we need—God Almighty
rewarder: one who pays wages
diligently seek: search for carefully

What does this say about Christ's role in giving us faith? What does this practically mean?

Read Hebrews 12:1–2:

Jesus, Founder and Perfecter of Our Faith

12 Therefore, since we are surrounded by so great a cloud of witnesses, let us also lay aside every weight, and sin which clings so closely, and let us run with endurance the race that is set before us, ² looking to Jesus, the founder and perfecter of our faith, who for the joy that was set before him endured the cross, despising the shame, and is seated at the right hand of the throne of God.

_____

_____

_____

_____

_____

Christ is the author and the completer, the finisher of faith. How does He author Faith? He speaks it and says something specifically about our issue. Father, I have a problem. I'm in adversity. What do you have to say about this? What is your word to me, God? (We'll talk more about that later–about getting to clarity.)

And then His next question is: Do you believe in certainty? And your answer is usually no. He says then that His work is to take you to certainty. Your role is to stay with Him as He finishes taking you to belief in what He has spoken, and that He will use testing to refine and take you to finishing.

Word Definitions: **author:** one that takes the lead in anything and thus affords an example, a predecessor in a matter, pioneer

finisher: a perfector, one who has in his own person raised faith to its perfection and so set before us the highest example of faith

How do we receive and process faith? How is this done practically?

Read Romans 10:17:

¹⁷ So faith comes from hearing, and hearing through the word of Christ.

_____

_____

_____

_____

_____

As He gives us faith—finishes our faith—the Biblical truth is that faith comes from hearing what He says—hearing from the Word of God. So, as you listen to His promises, your role is to diligently seek Him, stay in the Word until they, His promises, become certain. Do you have certainty?

The two issues are:

1. Do you even care? Do you wish to go to Him for Him to author faith? Most people don't. That's why they never get anywhere. They're always frustrated, and they're always experiencing adversity because they don't even care to hear what God has to say. And God saying, well, you're wandering around with all this adversity, and you don't even care what I have to say to resolve it. And there's nothing I can do other than to let you experience all these different causes of adversity. And you don't even know what's going on other than that you are experiencing pain, difficulty, and stress. And you're digging yourself deeper and deeper and deeper into holes. You ultimately fight each other, divorce each other, cause conflict, makes stupid mistakes, get yourself in more trouble and have more problems, etc.

2. You blame God when something doesn't come to pass. You are not willing to let Him finish taking you to faith, to certainty. You heard what He had to say, but when you fail the test of faith, when the circumstances go south, you go back to doubt and trying to resolve it on your own. You've heard it, and you've been processing it in the Word. And you come to a point where you

think, you know what, I think I believe this. And He's going to say, well, let's go prove it out in the circumstances that have or will go south on you. Now, is it to punish you? No. Is it to beat you up? No. It's only to prove it out, to determine if you believe with certainty. Will you fail the test? If you fail the test, you go back to worry, anxiety, or, oh my gosh, it isn't going to happen because I don't really believe this. He reminds us to stay with Him because He hasn't finished rewarding you with faith. You may think you are finished or that He is showing us that we are finished, but we are not. The worst thing you can do is think you're finished and then quit. It is for this reason that He has given us this test of faith. The testing is to reveal that we must continue to stay with Him so that He can finish taking us to certainty and giving us faith to believe. It is then that He can fulfill what He has spoken.

Word Definition: **Word:** Rhema

Example of testing: Abraham:

In these two sets of verses, what does it reveal about the faith of Abraham? Based upon Abraham's life, what do we know about his struggle with faith? What did he do well and no so well? Why is this so important in our life of faith?

Read Romans 4:17–21:

[17] as it is written, "I have made you the father of many nations"—in the presence of the God in whom he believed, who gives life to the dead and calls into existence the things that do not exist. [18] In hope he believed against hope, that he should become the father of many nations, as he had been told, "So shall your offspring be." [19] He did not weaken in faith when he considered his own body, which was as good as dead (since he was about a hundred years old), or when he considered the barrenness[a] of Sarah's womb. [20] No unbelief made him waver concerning the promise of God, but he grew strong in his faith as he gave glory to God, [21] fully convinced that God was able to do what he had promised.

_____

_____

_____

_____

_____

LESSON 2:
TYPES AND CAUSES OF REAL ADVERSITY

Read Genesis 22:1–18:

The Sacrifice of Isaac

22 After these things God tested Abraham and said to him, "Abraham!" And he said, "Here I am." ² He said, "Take your son, your only son Isaac, whom you love, and go to the land of Moriah, and offer him there as a burnt offering on one of the mountains of which I shall tell you." ³ So Abraham rose early in the morning, saddled his donkey, and took two of his young men with him, and his son Isaac. And he cut the wood for the burnt offering and arose and went to the place of which God had told him. ⁴ On the third day Abraham lifted up his eyes and saw the place from afar. ⁵ Then Abraham said to his young men, "Stay here with the donkey; I and the boy[a] will go over there and worship and come again to you."⁶ And Abraham took the wood of the burnt offering and laid it on Isaac his son. And he took in his hand the fire and the knife. So they went both of them together. ⁷ And Isaac said to his father Abraham, "My father!" And he said, "Here I am, my son." He said, "Behold, the fire and the wood, but where is the lamb for a burnt offering?" ⁸ Abraham said, "God will provide for himself the lamb for a burnt offering, my son." So they went both of them together.

⁹ When they came to the place of which God had told him, Abraham built the altar there and laid the wood in order and bound Isaac his son and laid him on the altar, on top of the wood. ¹⁰ Then Abraham reached out his hand and took the knife to slaughter his son. ¹¹ But the angel of the Lord called to him from heaven and said, "Abraham, Abraham!" And he said, "Here I am." ¹² He said, "Do not lay your hand on the boy or do anything to him, for now I know that you fear God, seeing you have not withheld your son, your only son, from me." ¹³ And Abraham lifted up his eyes and looked, and behold, behind him was a ram, caught in a thicket by his horns. And Abraham went and took the ram and offered it up as a burnt offering instead of his son. ¹⁴ So Abraham called the name of that place, "The Lord will provide";[b] as it is said to this day, "On the mount of the Lord it shall be provided."[c]

¹⁵ And the angel of the Lord called to Abraham a second time from heaven¹⁶ and said, "By myself I have sworn, declares the Lord, because you have done this and have not withheld your son, your only son, ¹⁷ I will surely bless you, and I will surely multiply your offspring as the stars of heaven and as the sand that is on the seashore. And your offspring shall possess the gate of his[d] enemies,¹⁸ and in your offspring shall all the nations of the earth be blessed, because you have obeyed my voice."

LESSON 2:
TYPES AND CAUSES OF REAL ADVERSITY

_____

_____

_____

_____

_____

Abraham was characterized in Scripture as a great man of faith who believed, contrary to hope in hope, stayed with it and became the father of many nations. As we look at Abraham's life and look at the events of his life, would we consider him a great man of faith. No. Why not?

Because he attempted to give his wife away several times. When the promise wasn't being fulfilled, he and Sarah decided to take care of it on their own and have a son with Sarah's handmaid, Hagar. Did God prevent them? No. He didn't step in and say: I'm absolutely not going to let you do that. It is always by our choice. God does give us promises (what He speaks). Then, it becomes a question of faith.

In this situation, Abraham and Sarah did not believe it. They decided to take care of this themselves and made a fundamental mistake regarding faith: They didn't go back to God and say, you know, it's not really happening. Should we just do this, or is there another way? And then God would have told him, no, you wait. Interestingly enough, it actually happens later, 13 years later, when God reiterates the promise. And here's what Abraham says. "I already have a child. So just use that guy. Just use him." To which, God refuses. God also says that Abraham is going to have to throw that son out because he's not the son of the promise. Abraham says, "Do you realize that Sarah's barren, she's in menopause, she can't have a baby. And I can't possibly have any sperm left. I'm done. Do you understand that?" And God says, "Does that prevent me from fulfilling what I said? The promise will be fulfilled. Are you going to believe me?" And, of course, this is where this whole verse comes to life. Abraham says, "Yes." He believed at that moment. The good thing Abraham did the whole time was that he stayed with God, even though he failed, he stayed in the process of receiving faith. This comes from hearing, and hearing comes from the Word.

Abraham became fully convinced that what God had promised He was able to perform, and God gave him the faith to believe it. The key was to stay with Him, stay with Him, stay with Him, even through all of our ridiculous failures. Abraham stayed with Him, and God was able to fully persuade him, which is His role. He also tested him along the way even as he stayed with Him. He did this until his faith was persuaded.

And then we know in Genesis, after he has Isaac, the son of promise, he is given the big test. God tells him to sacrifice, to kill his son, to eliminate the very promise He gave him. And Abraham, at that point, is confused. But still, he agrees. He says to a servant that he and the boy will return together from the mountain. By the way, you can read in Hebrews 11:19 his thought. I guess God's going to resurrect him. Now, think about that. There's never been a resurrection. He just says, I guess he's going to resurrect him, and we're going to come back. And, of course, God substitutes the lamb instead of the sacrifice, which is the symbol of Christ's substitution for our death. In Genesis 22:15, the angel of the Lord called Abraham a second time from out of heaven and said, "By myself I have sworn, declares the Lord, because you have done this and have not withheld your son, you willingly passed the test, and will receive the blessing. I will bless you and multiply, and I will multiply your descendants as the stars of Heaven, as the sand of the seashore and your descendants shall possess the gates of the enemies, and in your offspring all the nations of the Earth shall be blessed.

As we go into Galatians, he says that Christ is a recipient of the promise at the Covenant. He's going to bless us to make a blessing. He's going to give it to every believer individually, and they're going to be the recipients as they walk in Christ, which is the ability to overcome adversity, all because Abraham finally got there.

Word Definitions: **will provide:** to see, look at, inspect, perceive, consider, have vision
withhold: restrain, hold back, keep in check, refrain, to withhold, keep back, keep for oneself, keep from, hold in check, spare, reserve
obey: to hear, listen to, to hear (perceive by ear), to hear of or concerning, to hear (have power to hear), to hear with attention or interest, listen to
hope: expectation of good
believe: to think to be true, to be persuaded of, to credit, place confidence in
faith: conviction of the truth of anything, belief; in the conviction or belief respecting man's relationship to God and divine things, generally with the included idea of trust and holy fervor born of faith and joined with it, of the thing believed, to credit, have confidence
not waver: to be at variance with one's self, hesitate, doubt
assured: to make one certain
to persuade: convince one, to be persuaded, persuaded, fully convinced or assured
perform: to a promise

LESSON 3:
CAUSES OF ADVERSITY (CONTINUED)

> "Only the Vinedresser
> (the Father) knows
> exactly how much and
> where to prune."

PRUNING

This is entirely God's work; and is intended to cut back our activities and involvements, so that His desired fruit is produced. We, by becoming too involved and burdened by too many things to do, wind up having little or no fruit. Thus, God will bring adversity in what we are doing, so that we realize we are doing too much; and need to let him rearrange our life and create space and margin for us to receive the needed sunlight (the Son) and the needed water (the Holy Spirit) to enjoy being a branch and producing much (but not too much) high-quality fruit.

1. PRUNING (CUTTING BACK GROWTH OF THE BRANCH THAT IS GETTING TOO BIG TO PRODUCE FRUIT):

   a. Only healthy branches that are capable of bearing fruit are pruned. Unless pruned properly, pruning can actually cause the branch to die and have to be discarded; and only the vinedresser knows how to do it. Each branch is individual, so there is no one system for all branches. If pruned too much or too little, there will be no fruit. It has to be exactly what is needed for that particular branch. To protect from expected adversity (less than normal rain, potential frost, heat, wind, etc.), the location of the pruning is exact, so as to allow the branch to survive the adversity. Again, only the vinedresser knows this, and if not done properly, this incorrect pruning will result in the branch dying, not because of too little or too much, but because it's done in the wrong location.

   Key Revelation: Only the Vinedresser (the Father) knows exactly how much and where to prune. If we try to do this ourselves; or allow others to do this who are not the Vinedresser (churches, pastors, advisors, friends, spouses, etc.), we will make mistakes and actually accelerate our becoming useless and bearing no fruit.

b. The pruning has to be such that the branches and the leaves that will come and be continually pruned must have plenty of sun (SON) and water (HOLY SPIRIT) to be able to thrive. If after the initial pruning it starts to get too big (crowding as it flourishes, particularly in the center of the vine), it blocks the sunlight and water from the branches. Then as they get too big (although they are actually very healthy), the overgrowth then diminishes their ability to receive what is needed to thrive, and they shrink and then do not produce fruit.

c. After the initial pruning, the branches grow "shoots" from which the grapes ultimately are created and grow in bunches. As these shoots begin to grow, the vinedresser prunes the shoots right away (just after they pop out) so that there is plenty of space for the sunlight and water. The pruning, both initially and as the branch grows itself and sprouts shoots, is required to provide plenty of open space for the sunlight and rain to reach the branches, the leaves, and soak into the dirt that is necessary for strength of the vine.

Key Revelation: Pruning is ongoing and is geared to create space for sunlight and water, which are the sources of life. This is in addition to the primary reason of having the branch not get so big that the sap can't get through the branch into the fruit and so that water (Holy Spirit) is not absorbed by the branch resulting in no fruit. The Covenant: Blessed to become a blessing by giving it away. Our abiding is to fully allow, cooperate with, and desire the Father to prune back our activities (all the stuff we are doing), so that we can receive plenty of the Son and the Holy Spirit to produce His desired fruit. Without this space, the growth that seems really good to us (and measured as good by the world and even by the church) actually causes us to dry up, wither, and have no fruit. This describes us so well in becoming weary, worn out, even burned out with our good activities. We all need to pay attention to this big invitation by the Father to cut back, cut back, cut back. Do not think it is disappointing to God or being selfish. On the contrary, it is His perfect will for the fruit He plans and desires.

2. FRUIT: This one caught us by surprise. If the fruit (bunches of grapes) on the branches is so much so that it touches each other, they rot, become mushy, and are worthless. This "touching of bunches of grapes" does not allow the air needed for the grapes to continue its proper completion; and through this lack of air, they cause each other to rot. The fruit also needs "space," or it becomes worthless.

Key revelation: We always thought that much fruit meant as much fruit as possible and seems like that would be a good thing. Not so. When the fruit gets too much, it causes all of what's on that branch to rot. Wow, even the fruit needs to be managed and given plenty of space. Thus, we are not in any way to view the magnitude of our fruit as our responsibility or think that more is better. Rather, it is about what the Vinedresser desires and trusting that He knows what is optimal for us. Our fruit is to be discrete, and thus, not all forced together making it seem even bigger. Further, that the fruit is individual so having large groups where there is no space for the fruit to thrive causes the very fruit produced to rot and be worthless. This means to us that we will not actually know the fruit that God brings through our being faithful and just abiding, but by allowing Him to prune and bring His desired fruit. We believe this speaks to multiplication and that our real ministry fruit is helping those who God brings across our path to experience us receiving the amazing fruit of transformation and supernatural work. They themselves then want to get connected to the Vine and learn to abide, as well as to learn the lessons of pruning through space and margin. It is a big reorientation of our role, our willingness to let the Father prune us for this space and margin and understand that the very fruit of those who become fruit is produced for them to get connected with others and enjoy the life of abiding. This is very profound, but not easy to grasp.

What do these verses state about pruning? What happens when branches are pruned? Why?

Read John 15:1–5:

I Am the True Vine

15 "I am the true vine, and my Father is the vinedresser. [2] Every branch in me that does not bear fruit he takes away, and every branch that does bear fruit he prunes, that it may bear more fruit. [3] Already you are clean because of the word that I have spoken to you. [4] Abide in me, and I in you. As the branch cannot bear fruit by itself, unless it abides in the vine, neither can you, unless you abide in me. [5] I am the vine; you are the branches. Whoever abides in me and I in him, he it is that bears much fruit, for apart from me you can do nothing.

_____

_____

_____

_____

_____

Christ states that He's going to prune back those branches that are bearing fruit in order to bear more fruit, which means for us He is going to cut back, cut back, cut back, not allowing us to keep doing more in our life. We've got to think of the simplicity of margin.

Do you have space in your life for freedom, for things that are open? Are you doing too much? Because at the end of the day, you are tired. Are you late for meetings because you've always got too much to do? Do you give your projects half effort because you have to go to the next thing? Do you not have time for your spouse, and are you not enjoying things? Is your physical life getting out of hand because you don't have time for it or no longer actually really rest? So, it's margin. Are you relaxed? Are you having time for the things that God wants you to have time for, which is a relaxed, joyful life?

Word Definitions:

bear: bring forth, produce

prune: cleanse of filth, impurity, etc., to prune trees and vines from useless shoots

Who is responsible for pruning? How does He do this?

Read Hebrews 13:20–21:

Benediction

[20] Now may the God of peace who brought again from the dead our Lord Jesus, the great shepherd of the sheep, by the blood of the eternal covenant, [21] equip you with everything good that you may do his will, working in us[a] that which is pleasing in his sight, through Jesus Christ, to whom be glory forever and ever. Amen.

_____

_____

_____

_____

_____

God is going to equip you to do His will. He has planned the very good work ahead on His path for you. So, let Him equip you to set forth the work. Let Him choose and let Him show you what to do. And He says, it's about life and what He wants you to enjoy. And it will include us receiving and giving it away. But it is always as He so ordains at the moment—what is the most important thing on His path for you to have margin and bear fruit—so perhaps to spend time with your children or your wife so that your marriage doesn't become unhealthy. He wants us to strengthen our life so that the fruit will come from that. Perhaps we need to go work on that or our business. Or, He would like to reorganize the time you spend at work. He will help you decide if it's way too much. How could you operate in your business with your people? Are you doing the work you should be doing? He's going to give you wisdom. He's going to share with you what it is that it looks like to create margin in your life. Be willing to let Him prune you so you can bear the fruit that He has planned.

Word Definitions:

equip: to render, (i.e., to fit, sound, complete, to mend what has been broken), to repair, to fit out, put in order, arrange, adjust, to fit or frame for one's self, prepare
well pleasing: acceptable

What does He say about not being entangled in civilian affairs? What does this mean practically to us as believers and followers of Christ?

Read 2 Timothy 2:1–7:

A Good Soldier of Christ Jesus
2 then, my child, be strengthened by the grace that is in Christ Jesus, [2] and what you have heard from me in the presence of many witnesses entrust to faithful men,[a] who will be able to teach others also. [3] Share in suffering as a good soldier of Christ Jesus. [4] No soldier gets entangled in civilian pursuits, since his aim is to please the one who enlisted him. [5] An athlete is not crowned unless he competes according to the rules. [6] It is the hard-working farmer who ought to have the first share of the crops. [7] Think over what I say, for the Lord will give you understanding in everything.

_____

_____

_____

_____

_____

He basically gives us this interesting statement to not get entangled in things that He has not given you to do. So, he who is in the military does not get involved in outside activities since they have not been assigned by his commanding officer. He's a soldier. He doesn't go do other things. Why not? Because they are not his responsibility. The officer has given him orders: you go do this and you don't have the privilege of going to do what you decide may be important outside of those orders. There is no entanglement where we're trying to juggle the orders of the Master and the things that we've decided we want to do to. There is no pressure because we have no burden to figure out any entanglements. For us, we try to do too much and get involved in entanglement—mental entanglements, energy entanglements. And you get tired and weary and struggle. And, by the way, nothing gets done well, and you're just going from thing to thing to thing. And you're saying, well, look at all the stuff I'm doing. And the truth is you're having no fruit (which we tend to define as activity, but is not fruit, and especially not God's fruit).

How often do you have to prune? All the time. Our margin is not permanent, but rather continually has to be evaluated (because branches grow and need pruning) and our lives cut back so we maintain our sweet spots, our margin that He ordains.

Are you living in joy? Do you have margin and time for rest? Are you experiencing freedom? And the things that you're involved in, are they God's? Are you experiencing fruit? Constantly reevaluate this and make adjustments as necessary.

Word Definition: **to entangle:** to inweave, to involve in business, occupation

SELF-CENTEREDNESS

What are the consequences of our self-centeredness? Why is this significant to our lives? Why are we self-centered?

Read James 1:12–18:

12 Blessed is the man who remains steadfast under trial, for when he has stood the test he will receive the crown of life, which God has promised to those who love him. 13 Let no one say when he is tempted, "I am being tempted by God," for God cannot be tempted with evil, and he himself tempts no one. 14 But each person is tempted when he is lured and enticed by his own desire. 15 Then desire when it has conceived gives birth to sin, and sin when it is fully grown brings forth death.

16 Do not be deceived, my beloved brothers. 17 Every good gift and every perfect gift is from above, coming down from the Father of lights, with whom there is no variation or shadow due to change.[a] 18 Of his own will he brought us forth by the word of truth, that we should be a kind of firstfruits of his creatures.

_____

_____

_____

_____

_____

We do have consequences (i.e., adversity if we act in self-centeredness and not follow God). You get drawn away by your selfish, lousy choices. You are questioning whether or not something is a good idea. This is called temptation. And the enemy is using that to draw us away from God and to sin, to use our own will (flesh) and decide things on our own. And you walk right out into the world, the kingdom of the world, and you're getting whacked. Why? Because you're not in God's will, and you've decided that you know better.

When you decide that you're going to go do this on your own, you lose your protection and your ability for God to give you the beautiful life He has planned for you. You walk out into enemy territory without protection. There's something about enemy territory. What's it like? It is a place of entropy: steal, kill, and destroy, and it's destroying your life circumstantially. But it was caused because you went out there on your own without protection, you walked out of God's Kingdom.

Word Definitions:

temptation: in a bad sense, to test one maliciously, craftily to put to the proof his feelings or judgments, to try or test one's faith, virtue, character, by enticement to sin, to solicit to sin, to tempt, of the temptations of the devil

evils: of a bad nature, not such as it ought to be, of a mode of thinking, feeling, acting, base, wrong, wicked, troublesome, injurious, pernicious, destructive, baneful

selfish desires: desire, craving, longing, desire for what is forbidden, lust

drawn away: to draw out metaph. lure forth: in hunting and fishing as game is lured from its hiding place, so man by lure is allured from the safety of self-restraint to sin. In James 1:14, the language of the hunting is transferred to the seduction of a harlot

being enticed: to bait, catch by a bait, metaph. to beguile by banishments, allure, entice, deceive

What causes our conflicts and quarrels? Underneath this is a more profound reason for difficulties. What are they? Why do we as believers experience these?

Read James 4:1–5:

Warning Against Worldliness

4 What causes quarrels and what causes fights among you? Is it not this, that your passions[a] are at war within you?[b] 2 You desire and do not have, so you murder. You covet and cannot obtain, so you fight and quarrel. You do not have, because you do not ask. 3 You ask and do not receive, because you ask wrongly, to spend it on your passions. 4 You adulterous people![c] Do you not know that friendship with the world is enmity with God? Therefore whoever wishes to be a friend of the world makes himself an enemy of God. 5 Or do you suppose it is to no purpose that the Scripture says, "He yearns jealously over the spirit that he has made to dwell in us"?

_____

_____

_____

_____

_____

This states that we are experiencing fighting, that we are having conflict. Things aren't working well. And it is because you're selfish, and you're dealing with other selfish people. He says no wonder things aren't going well. You're experiencing this adversity because you're self-centered.

Further, there are two issues:

1. You don't even ask God for answers because you've assumed everything is God's will. It must be from God. He says this is not so. You didn't even ask Him.

2. Those who do ask God do so with selfish desires, so your prayer is completely backwards. How are you praying? Gimme, gimme, gimme: I want, I want, I want You to bless my plan. I've got a problem. Solve my problem and I'll see You later. You haven't even discussed anything that He already told you. The reason you have a problem is because you're self-centered. He says, "I can't solve this problem because you aren't allowing me to solve this problem."

Word Definitions:

quarrels: dispute, strife

conflicts: of persons at variance, disputants etc., strife, contention

passions: desires for pleasure

to have a desire for: long for, to desire; to lust after

covet: desire earnestly, pursue, to desire one earnestly, to strive after, busy one's self about him, to exert one's self for one (that he may not be torn from me)

spend it on yourself: waste, squander, consume

What are the reasons we are considered foolish? What are the consequences?

Read Proverbs 18:1–2:

18 Whoever isolates himself seeks his own desire;
   he breaks out against all sound judgment.
² A fool takes no pleasure in understanding,
   but only in expressing his opinion.

_____

_____

_____

_____

_____

You seek your own desire and interestingly enough, you rage against sound judgment and wisdom because you are a fool. And you've gotten completely upside down and wonder how come God doesn't answer. You're so stuck on your own, in your way, you don't even listen to anything that God has to offer you. God calls you a fool because you're stubborn. You've already decided. His words don't fit the paradigm of what you want to do. And so, you are not willing to go any farther. This leaves you struggling with your adversity which you yourself are causing.

Word Definitions:

seeks his own desire: demands, lust, appetite, covetousness
rages: to break out (in contention)
wisdom: sound knowledge, success, sound or efficient wisdom, abiding success
fool: stupid fellow, dullard, simpleton, arrogant one
no delight: no pleasure in
understanding: insight

What problem does haste cause? Why do we tend to go too fast?

Read Proverbs 19:2–3:

2 Desire[a] without knowledge is not good,
  and whoever makes haste with his feet misses his way.
3 When a man's folly brings his way to ruin,
  his heart rages against the Lord.

_____

_____

_____

_____

_____

He says another big contributor to experiencing self-centered adversity is that we are going so fast that we don't even have a chance to listen to what God has to say or to receive His insight. Things continue not to go well. So, you live in anxiety, fear, and worry because you don't see a way out of it. And even though He says He can give you a way out of it, you want immediate results so try to fix things yourself. But then, of course, nothing is taken care of, so you fret some more.

Word Definitions: **haste:** press, be pressed, make haste, urge, be narrow

foolishness: folly

twist: pervert, distort, overturn, ruin

to fret: be sad, be wroth, be vexed, be enraged, be out of humor

As a believer, we do attempt to spend time in the Word, but often it has no affect and contributes to our adversity. Why is this and what does this look like in our lives?

Read Mark 4:13–19:

13 And he said to them, "Do you not understand this parable? How then will you understand all the parables? 14 The sower sows the word. 15 And these are the ones along the path, where the word is sown: when they hear, Satan immediately comes and takes away the word that is sown in them. 16 And these are the ones sown on rocky ground: the ones who, when they hear the word, immediately receive it with joy. 17 And they have no root in themselves, but endure for a while; then, when tribulation or persecution arises on account of the word, immediately they fall away.[a] 18 And others are the ones sown among thorns. They are those who hear the word, 19 but the cares of the world and the deceitfulness of riches and the desires for other things enter in and choke the word, and it proves unfruitful.

_____

_____

_____

_____

_____

In the situation you are attempting to seek some answers from God, and are in the Word of God, but are selfish. You don't stay with it and so it never bears fruit; it never gets there because you immediately have a little bit of it, but stop spending further time with it, so the enemy just takes that away. How easy for the enemy! You have a little bit of joy, but then the moment adversity comes, you stop pursuing God.

And you quit immediately, "I knew this was going to happen because that's been my experience. I know the way God operates. I don't really believe God is going to take care of this. I knew this was going to happen." So, you quit, fail, and fall away.

In other situations, you're so wrapped up in the cares of the world, the deceitfulness, or your own desires that you choke out God's involvement. You've allowed yourself to become so immersed and intermingled in the world, it just chokes out the Word. You may have spent some time in the Word, but then always drift back to the world and then encounter the destructive way of the world, which you have accepted as normal.

Word Definitions:

root: from a prime root, a sprout, shoot

tribulations: pressing, pressing together, pressure, metaph. oppression, affliction, distress, straits

fall away: to cause a person to begin to distrust and desert one whom he ought to trust and obey

deceit: deceitfulness

desire: craving, longing, desire for what is forbidden, lust

choke: to press round or throng one so as almost to suffocate him

unfruitful: metaph. without fruit, barren, not yielding what it ought to yield

In these verses, what are the scenarios that cause adversity? What do these look like in our lives?

Read Psalm 107:4–5; 10–12; 17–18:

[4] Some wandered in desert wastes,
  finding no way to a city to dwell in;
[5] hungry and thirsty,
  their soul fainted within them.

[10] Some sat in darkness and in the shadow of death,
  prisoners in affliction and in irons,
[11] for they had rebelled against the words of God,
  and spurned the counsel of the Most High.
[12] So he bowed their hearts down with hard labor;
  they fell down, with none to help.

> ¹⁷ Some were fools through their sinful ways,
>   and because of their iniquities suffered affliction;
> ¹⁸ they loathed any kind of food,
>   and they drew near to the gates of death.

_____

_____

_____

_____

_____

In these verses, we see three scenarios where selfishness has caused adversity:

1. Some wandered in the desert wastelands, finding no way to a city where they could live. So, they were hungry and thirsty, and their lives wasted away.

2. Some sat in darkness and the deepest gloom, prisoners suffering in iron chains, but they had rebelled against the Word of God and despised the council of the Most High. So, He subjected them to bitter labor. They stumbled, and there was no one to help.

3. Some came forth from their rebellious ways and suffered affliction because of their iniquities. They loathed all food and drew near the gates of death.

    So, when I'm just trying to figure this out on my own, sitting in darkness, I decide this is the way it's supposed to be. Then I go through adversity, and I don't know why. And I guess this is it, or I'm just rebellious and I don't care. It's all self-centered, not going to God, which is a cause of winding up in adversity, but I still don't really care. In all of these, I'm causing this adversity myself because I'm not willing to seek God. This brings worldly, destructive consequences.

Word Definitions: **wander:** go astray, err, stagger, to wander about (physically)
darkness: obscurity
rebellious: to be contentious, be rebellious, be refractory, be disobedient towards, be rebellious against iniquity: perversity, depravity, guilt or punishment of iniquity
transgression: rebellion

What does being in the carnal mean? What are the consequences of being in the carnal? Why is this so significant to our problems of adversity?

> **Read Romans 8:5–8:**
>
> [5] For those who live according to the flesh set their minds on the things of the flesh, but those who live according to the Spirit set their minds on the things of the Spirit. [6] For to set the mind on the flesh is death, but to set the mind on the Spirit is life and peace. [7] For the mind that is set on the flesh is hostile to God, for it does not submit to God's law; indeed, it cannot. [8] Those who are in the flesh cannot please God.

_____

_____

_____

_____

_____

When we are carnally minded as a believer (self-centered, I know better, I set my mind on what I want, and I'm going to pursue what I want), we have consequences. I have the Holy Spirit, but I'm deciding to live in the flesh, the spirit of selfishness. What are the three consequences?

1. **Death.** I've separated myself from the very power of the Spirit, which can lead me into overcoming. I act as if it doesn't exist and go back to the carnal without the power of the Spirit.

2. **Enmity against God.** I'm working against the purposes of God, and therefore, I'm going to have no assistance from God, so I'm not cooperating with God. I'm not asking God to resolve it. I'm actually working against Him. The only one who can resolve it, I'm working against. I'm in this conundrum. I've got a problem. I need a solution. And God is saying the only one who can solve it is Him. But in order for Him to work, I'm going to have to come with Him where He sits in the Kingdom and surrender. We must let Him be king. If you decide not to walk with Him by default, you're back into the flesh. And the flesh is, again, self-centeredness, which, by the way, is causing this adversity. When that occurs:

3. You cannot please God. That's pretty strong. But these consequences are real, and your selfishness is causing your adversity.

There are consequences to living in the carnal (division, selfishness); as believers in the carnal, we have three consequences: death of the Spirit (go back as it was with Adam and Eve where they lost the Spirit from their essence). As a believer who has the Holy Spirit, we basically shut off the power and relationship of the Spirit – as if it is dead; enmity against God, which means we are working against the will of God and ultimately means having the Father as an enemy (How is that going to work for you?); and, then we come to the point where we cannot please God. Displeasing God invites discipline (because He wants us to live in beautiful relationship with Him and receive all the benefits of the abundant life of the Kingdom).

Word Definitions: **flesh:** the sensuous nature of man, "the animal nature"; the animal nature with cravings which incite to sin, carnal
death: thickest darkness
enmity: hostile, hating, and opposing another
cannot please: not be able to have power, whether by virtue of one's own ability and resources, or of a state of mind, or through favorable circumstances, does not accommodate the desires of God

What does being selfish cause? How is chasing riches selfish? What does that mean when we are to work and earn money and need money to function in life?

Read 1 Timothy 6:9–10:

[9] But those who desire to be rich fall into temptation, into a snare, into many senseless and harmful desires that plunge people into ruin and destruction. [10] For the love of money is a root of all kinds of evils. It is through this craving that some have wandered away from the faith and pierced themselves with many pangs.

_____

_____

_____

_____

_____

LESSON 3:
CAUSES OF ADVERSITY (CONTINUED)

Believers have faith, but because they have strayed (stopped walking in faith) because of their selfishness, they fell into all kinds of trouble. They weren't willing to seek God; they decided they would rather pursue riches over God. But remember the truth that we absolutely cannot serve God and money at the same time. This will result in adversity which is simply foolishness.

Word Definitions: **desiring:** to will deliberately, have a purpose, be minded, willing as an affection, to desire

rich: to have abundance of outward possessions

temptation: rebellion against God, by which His power and justice are, as it were, put to the proof and challenged to show themselves

snare: trap, noose, of snares in which birds are entangled and caught, implies unexpectedly, suddenly, because birds and beasts are caught unaware

foolish: not understood, unintelligible, not understanding, unwise

harmful: hurtful, injurious; ruin, destroy

What causes separation from God? Why? What does this look like for us personally?

Read Isaiah 59:1–2:

Evil and Oppression

59 Behold, the Lord's hand is not shortened, that it cannot save,
  or his ear dull, that it cannot hear;
² but your iniquities have made a separation
  between you and your God,
and your sins have hidden his face from you
  so that he does not hear.

_____

_____

_____

_____

_____

This is very straightforward. This is not about things we do, but unwillingness to walk with Him. Separation comes when we refuse to walk with Him. You choose to go your own way, which is going back to the original issue, which caused Satan to get control, which is what happened with Adam and Eve. They exercised their self-will, thinking they knew better. This is exactly what happened to Satan when he fell in the first place. It's always about the will. Are you going to follow God or not? It's always that simple choice. And when you choose not to, He'll give you that permission. But then realize, you will have consequences to that. The first major consequence, when Adam and Eve decided to be disobedient was that they handed over authority to Satan. That authority now affects all of us. Did God decide that He'd force His will upon us? He did not, even though He knew the consequence would affect mankind for all of history.

The consequences accrue to your choice. You can be the cause of the consequences; your selfishness can cause your own adversity. It wasn't God, and it was not Satan per se. It was you who caused it. Because of your unwillingness to follow God.

Word Definitions: **iniquity:** perversity, depravity, guilt or punishment of iniquity
separate: to divide, sever, to separate, set apart

LESSON 4:
CAUSES OF ADVERSITY (CONTINUED)

DISCIPLINE

What do these verses tell us about God's purpose in discipline? What causes discipline? How does this apply to us?

> **Read Hebrews 12:5–7:**
>
> [5] And have you forgotten the exhortation that addresses you as sons?
> "My son, do not regard lightly the discipline of the Lord,
>   nor be weary when reproved by him.
> [6] For the Lord disciplines the one he loves,
>   and chastises every son whom he receives."
> [7] It is for discipline that you have to endure. God is treating you as sons. For what son is there whom his father does not discipline?

_____

_____

_____

_____

_____

_____

_____

_____

" The Scriptures tell us not to be discouraged in situations where discipline is necessary."

The Scriptures tell us not to be discouraged in situations where discipline is necessary. For those of us who have children, why would we say that discipline is necessary? Because we need to keep guiding toward the behaviors that will ultimately bring them success. And, because we want a good life for them, they need to know right from wrong. If they are heading in the wrong way due to selfishness or some other reason, we bring them back from the darkness.

As parents, we instruct. And, while our children may agree with our instruction in the short term, perhaps they then don't follow the instruction. The natural result of this is some consequence.

And even though this is clear, they still do not follow the instruction, acting in rebellion. They don't care what you've told them and want to do it their own way. If they keep doing what you've just instructed them not to do, what's going to happen? It's going to get worse and worse and worse; because we actually do know better, which is why we share our wisdom with them in the first place. We do it because we love them and want them to have the best life possible. That's what He says: He who loves his son gives him instruction. But there's a time when they need discipline or chastening, this happens when they are being stubborn and are willfully disobeying.

Further, when the willfulness gets stronger (they understand that they are not following your instruction, but just do not care), then your discipline becomes harsher and more severe, and now there's a consequence to their action that you've added on top of what they're experiencing anyway. Why did you do it? What's the purpose? At that moment, they need correction so that they become obedient and enter into a better life. Hopefully they'll wake up and say, you know what, OK, I see it. I'm willing. I don't want to have more consequence. So regardless of my rebellion, I'm going to wake up and repent. I'll do it your way; I'll surrender my will to your will. That's the idea. The reason He says a father loves his child is so that they come back to the relationship and follow the solution to the best life possible. Because you know better than they do.

Word Definitions:
love: to welcome, to entertain, to be fond of, to love dearly
discipline: to train children, to be instructed or taught, to cause one to learn, to chastise, to chastise or castigate with words, to correct, of those who are molding the character of others by reproof and admonition
receive: to accept; of a son: to acknowledge as one's own
partaker: to be or to be made a partner
holiness: sanctity, God's nature

What is correction about? Why? Why is it necessary? How does it apply to us?

Read Proverbs 3:11–12:

[11] My son, do not despise the Lord's discipline
or be weary of his reproof,
[12] for the Lord reproves him whom he loves,
as a father the son in whom he delights.

_____

_____

_____

_____

_____

He states clearly that the purpose of correction is about the heart—that God wants you to receive it. It's going to be best for you if you receive it; to bring you back and set you on the right course. It's never to harm us or give us more pain. The purpose of all this is to bring you back. He's basically trying to say, "If I were you, I would be willing to receive it."

Word Definitions: **weary:** be grieved, loathe, abhor, feel a loathing or abhorrence or sickening dread
despise: reject, refuse
chastening: discipline, correction
corrects: to prove, decide, judge, rebuke, reprove, be right
love: affection for

What was the problem with the church? Why did it require discipline? What was offered? What does this mean to us?

Read Revelation 3:14–22:

To the Church in Laodicea
[14] "And to the angel of the church in Laodicea write: 'The words of the Amen, the faithful and true witness, the beginning of God's creation.

> [15] "'I know your works: you are neither cold nor hot. Would that you were either cold or hot! [16] So, because you are lukewarm, and neither hot nor cold, I will spit you out of my mouth. [17] For you say, I am rich, I have prospered, and I need nothing, not realizing that you are wretched, pitiable, poor, blind, and naked. [18] I counsel you to buy from me gold refined by fire, so that you may be rich, and white garments so that you may clothe yourself and the shame of your nakedness may not be seen, and salve to anoint your eyes, so that you may see. [19] Those whom I love, I reprove and discipline, so be zealous and repent. [20] Behold, I stand at the door and knock. If anyone hears my voice and opens the door, I will come in to him and eat with him, and he with me. [21] The one who conquers, I will grant him to sit with me on my throne, as I also conquered and sat down with my Father on his throne. [22] He who has an ear, let him hear what the Spirit says to the churches.'"

_____

_____

_____

_____

_____

Here, Christ is speaking to the church, not to unbelievers. He's saying He is unhappy with them because they're not following Him and have become lukewarm because they're operating in the flesh. They're operating on their own, He says, but since He loves us, He is going to chasten us, to correct us. He does this by standing at the door and knocking. He wants us to listen to what He has to say.

What, then, would our role be? To open the door! Because He says you must repent and be willing to open the door so that He can come in. You are going to go back to fellowship and are going to overcome your problem. All you must do is repent. Then He may discipline you. Why? Because you're not walking with Him, and He loves you so much that He needs to correct you.

Word Definitions: **to love:** to approve of; to like, sanction, to treat affectionately or kindly, to welcome, befriend

rebuke: to convict, refute, confute, generally with a suggestion of shame of the person, convict

discipline: to train children, to be instructed or taught, to cause one to learn, to chastise, to chastise or castigate with words, to correct, of those who are molding the character of others by reproof and admonition

Why did the psalmist appreciate being disciplined? What does it say about God's reasons for discipline? How does this apply to us?

Read Psalm 119:65–72:

Teth

⁶⁵ You have dealt well with your servant,
    O Lord, according to your word.
⁶⁶ Teach me good judgment and knowledge,
    for I believe in your commandments.
⁶⁷ Before I was afflicted I went astray,
    but now I keep your word.
⁶⁸ You are good and do good;
    teach me your statutes.
⁶⁹ The insolent smear me with lies,
    but with my whole heart I keep your precepts;
⁷⁰ their heart is unfeeling like fat,
    but I delight in your law.
⁷¹ It is good for me that I was afflicted,
    that I might learn your statutes.
⁷² The law of your mouth is better to me
    than thousands of gold and silver pieces.

_____

_____

_____

_____

_____

The psalmist states that he understands that it was good that God disciplined him. Why? Because then, he learned God's statutes and learned His ways, His instructions. He learned that God's way was better than his. He was living back in victory and overcoming. Even though he caused his own pain, He knew he needed God's correction to get back on the path toward repentance and ultimate victory. Once we have experienced the consequences of what we ourselves have caused, then God invites you to follow Him: He wants you to let Him come and resolve it. But if you refuse, because you think you know better, then He may need to make it worse. He may need to punish further, but all with the purpose of bringing you back to fellowship again.

Word Definitions: **to afflict:** oppress, humble, be afflicted, be bowed down

to teach: to be taught, be trained

JUDGEMENT

What are the reasons for judgment? What exactly is judgment? How does this apply to us?

Read Jeremiah 1:15–16:

[15] For behold, I am calling all the tribes of the kingdoms of the north, declares the Lord, and they shall come, and every one shall set his throne at the entrance of the gates of Jerusalem, against all its walls all around and against all the cities of Judah. [16] And I will declare my judgments against them, for all their evil in forsaking me. They have made offerings to other gods and worshiped the works of their own hands.

_____

_____

_____

_____

_____

When there is no response to the discipline, then God brings judgment—more severe consequences. He brings in judgment by using the things of the world against us. In this case, it was Babylonia. He's bringing judgment. Why? Wickedness: not following or checking in with God, and not being willing to seek God's answer in any way. Judgment is coming because they've refused the first call. He asked them to come back, but they wouldn't. So, He disciplined. Then He asked again. But they still refused as their hearts grew even harder and more wicked. They wanted to do everything their own way. Then, God says, okay, then what's next is going to be judgment. And it's going to be harsher, and it's going to be severe. For us, consequence may be a finality of something in our life, like a business or a financial issue or a relationship, and it's literally going to come to an end, with no way out from a natural perspective. You have faced a judgment.

The wonderful thing about the life of God is that He can still restore our life, which we'll see.

When somebody is having difficulty or experiencing significant stress and trouble, are they following God? Or are they cheating on their wife or cheating in business, or behaving dishonestly? They soon will find that things get worse and worse if they don't willingly repent and come back and see God. Remember, a believer who no longer cares will see God's judgment, because He never stops caring.

The heart of God would be for that person to come back to Him. There will be judgment and there may be a point where you'll wind up in an even worse predicament. Maybe then they'll say enough is enough and finally come back. But people's hearts can get harder and harder and harder to where they don't really care anymore about what God says or doesn't say and decide to do what they want to do. They then should expect God's judgment.

Word Definitions: **wickedness:** bad, evil (adjective), disagreeable, malignant, unpleasant, evil (giving pain, unhappiness, misery), displeasing, bad (of its kind—land, water, etc.), bad (of value), worse than, worst

judgment: act of deciding a case, place, court, seat of judgment, process, procedure, litigation (before judges), case, cause (presented for judgment), sentence, decision (of judgment), execution

What are further reasons for judgment? What are these practically in our lives?

Read Jeremiah 7:24–34:

24 But they did not obey or incline their ear, but walked in their own counsels and the stubbornness of their evil hearts, and went backward and not forward. 25 From the day that your fathers came out of the land of Egypt to this day, I have persistently sent all my servants the prophets to them, day after day. 26 Yet they did not listen to me or incline their ear, but stiffened their neck. They did worse than their fathers.

27 "So you shall speak all these words to them, but they will not listen to you. You shall call to them, but they will not answer you. 28 And you shall say to them, 'This is the nation that did not obey the voice of the Lord their God, and did not accept discipline; truth has perished; it is cut off from their lips.

29 "'Cut off your hair and cast it away;
  raise a lamentation on the bare heights,

> for the Lord has rejected and forsaken
>   the generation of his wrath.'
>
> The Valley of Slaughter
> [30] "For the sons of Judah have done evil in my sight, declares the Lord. They have set their detestable things in the house that is called by my name, to defile it. [31] And they have built the high places of Topheth, which is in the Valley of the Son of Hinnom, to burn their sons and their daughters in the fire, which I did not command, nor did it come into my mind. [32] Therefore, behold, the days are coming, declares the Lord, when it will no more be called Topheth, or the Valley of the Son of Hinnom, but the Valley of Slaughter; for they will bury in Topheth, because there is no room elsewhere. [33] And the dead bodies of this people will be food for the birds of the air, and for the beasts of the earth, and none will frighten them away. [34] And I will silence in the cities of Judah and in the streets of Jerusalem the voice of mirth and the voice of gladness, the voice of the bridegroom and the voice of the bride, for the land shall become a waste.

_____

_____

_____

_____

_____

Here we see further explanation for the judgment: They follow their own counsel, they're not listening to God, to truth. Their hearts are hard. They have abandoned anything God had to say, even when He has corrected them. What did they do with the correction? They rejected it. They received disciplined and instruction. But they didn't follow that. God tried again to correct them, but they rejected it. And now they've come to a place where all truth is gone, and their heart is now so hard that they can no longer see truth.

Is there a consequence to that? Yes. Things aren't going to go well. What you do not see is that God is trying to show you something.

God moved you through adversity, but you rejected Him. Then He took you through discipline, but you didn't care. He then moved to judgment, so things begin getting worse and worse and worse. Remember, the purpose of God's judgment is always: Are you willing to come back?

Word Definitions:

evil: bad, evil (adjective), disagreeable, malignant, unpleasant, evil (giving pain, unhappiness, misery), displeasing, bad (of its kind—land, water, etc.), bad (of value), worse than, worst

own counsel: counsel, plan, principal, device

not listen: to not hear, listen to, obey (verb), to hear (perceive by ear), to hear of or concerning, to hear (have power to hear), to hear with attention or interest, listen to

hardened: to be hard, be difficult

forsake: abandon; reject, despise, refuse

to cause to cease: put an end to, to exterminate, destroy

How do these "Christmas" verses describe Christ's government? What role does judgment have? Why is this important for us to live out?

Read Isaiah 9:6–7:

6 For to us a child is born,
   to us a son is given;
and the government shall be upon[a] his shoulder,
   and his name shall be called[b]
Wonderful Counselor, Mighty God,
   Everlasting Father, Prince of Peace.
7 Of the increase of his government and of peace
   there will be no end,
on the throne of David and over his kingdom,
   to establish it and to uphold it
with justice and with righteousness
   from this time forth and forevermore.
The zeal of the Lord of hosts will do this.

_____

_____

_____

_____

_____

He's the prince of peace–yes; wonderful counselor–yes; but He also says His government is going to operate in His Kingdom. And remember, His Word is absolute. It does operate and it operates with judgment. And justice. It's absolute. Justice will be served. You're either going to live with Him or not, and as we just learned, if you don't walk with Him, you put to death the Spirit. You're at enmity against Him, and you cannot please Him. And He says you're going to suffer consequences for that because His Word is a double-edged sword.

He invites you to the beautiful life that comes if you choose to follow Him. But it also will be that you'll suffer the consequences of it if you choose not to. But when you don't, He will invite you to return. Yes, He'll discipline you. Then, if you reject discipline, then God will bring judgment. This goes back to the truth of Jesus, when He states in John Chapter 12: "I haven't come to judge you. My words, My truth judges you." Why? Because justice is served. And this is an important understanding.

He wants to give us the beautiful life, but He can't do that automatically. When you're walking away from Him, when you're stubborn, when you're rebellious, when you're saying, I don't care, He will discipline you with an invitation to repent and return; and then if you further refuse, then He will bring judgment, but always with an invitation to repent and return so you can receive the great life He has planned for you.

He can't force you to come to Him. All He can do is offer it to you. If you decide to come back and want to process, He'll help you. But if you walk away, you walk away. He's not going to force you to return. He will bless you if you choose to walk into the truth, but as a parent loves the child, there are consequences to you walking away.

Word Definitions: **government:** rule, dominion
justice: righteousness, (in government), of judge, ruler, king, truthfulness
judgment: act of deciding a case, place, court, seat of judgment, process, procedure, litigation (before judges), case, cause (presented for judgment), sentence, decision (of judgment), execution

ATTACK OF SATAN:

How does this verse describe Satan? What does that mean in our lives?

Read 1 Peter 5:8:

⁸ Be sober-minded; be watchful. Your adversary the devil prowls around like a roaring lion, seeking someone to devour.

_____

_____

_____

_____

_____

Satan is like a lion walking about, looking to find who he can destroy. The world that he controls and has authority over is destruction; remember, he's steal, kill, and destroy. A lion hunts by just walking around and looking for prey; they're constantly seeking out or observing a weak one, the obvious one to devour. The enemy is relentless, always looking for targets. And of course, he's going to show us that, when you're in Christ, when you're in God, you're going to be less of a target. That doesn't mean we're not a target. But he's looking for weak targets.

Word Definitions:

adversary: opponent, an opponent in a suit of law, an adversary, enemy
prowl: to make one's way, progress; to make use of opportunities
seek: in order to find
devour: to swallow up, destroy

What are we fighting against? Why is this important to understand in our lives? What schemes do they use, and how do we experience these?

Read Ephesians 6:10–12:

The Whole Armor of God
¹⁰ Finally, be strong in the Lord and in the strength of his might. ¹¹ Put on the whole armor of God, that you may be able to stand against the schemes of the

---

> devil. [12] For we do not wrestle against flesh and blood, but against the rulers, against the authorities, against the cosmic powers over this present darkness, against the spiritual forces of evil in the heavenly places.

_____

_____

_____

_____

_____

In these verses, Paul states that we are not fighting against flesh and blood (other people) but fighting against the powers and principalities in the spiritual realm, the demonic who are having schemes. What's the scheme? It's a well thought-out plan, a well thought-out crafty trick evaluation of: How can I get to you? What can I do to get you to go to the flesh, the self, and move out of the protection of God? Remember, they're not God, they're not omnipresent, they're not omnipotent, they don't have every quality of God because they're not God. They're created beings. So, when he talks about the enemies prowling around, he's talking about the host of enemies prowling around because Satan is finite, but he's got lots of helpers and he talks about their structure, powers, principalities, host, how they're organized like a big corporation. They have field guys, and they're observing you. What are they looking for? Your weaknesses, and their corresponding cause and effect. When something happens to you, they learn how you will respond. You go to war, you go to fear, you go to anxiety, you go to anger, you go to frustration. How can they use your circumstances to get you to stop pursuing God and instead pursue your own devices, stop praying, stop abiding, or come up with your own solutions? That's where Satan's got the victory because he's way more powerful than you in the natural. In God, he's not—you are more powerful than him. So, the demonic are observing you with schemes and tricks.

It is for this reason that God says you've got to understand how to fight that battle. You've got to stay in the spiritual realm, because in the natural realm, you have no chance of overcoming Satan. The enemy is looking for opportunity, wondering the best way to attack to get you into his arena, which will put you into the world of destruction. He wants you to take your own first step, take that action of reaction, of anger, frustration. Take that action. And you've just stuck your hand in the tar. With him, you are now stuck, compounding your issue by 10. Satan will be pleased because you acted in the natural without considering the power you have in God. He does not want us going back to ask for God's peace and God's

LESSON 4:
CAUSES OF ADVERSITY (CONTINUED)

opinion. A lot of times Satan will say, don't do or say anything—don't ask for God's help. But it's always time for God to help you work things through the way He intended.

Word Definitions:

schemes: cunning arts, deceit, craft, trickery

wrestling: (a contest between two in which each endeavors to throw the other, and which is decided when the victor is able to hold his opponent down with his hand upon his neck), the term is transferred to the Christian's struggle with the power of evil

principality: rule, magistracy, of angels and demons

powers: one who possesses authority, a ruler, the leading and more powerful among created beings, superior to man, spiritual potentates

rulers: lord of the world, prince of this age, the devil and his demons

darkness: of ignorance respecting divine things and human duties, and the accompanying ungodliness and immorality, together with their consequent misery in hell

wickedness: full of labors, annoyances, hardships, pressed and harassed by labors, bringing toils, annoyances, perils; of a time full of peril to Christian faith and steadfastness; causing pain and trouble, bad, of a bad nature or condition, in a

physical sense: diseased or blind, in an ethical sense: evil wicked, bad

What is always with us? Why is this important to understand? How are we to approach this problem?

Read Matthew 13:36–43:

The Parable of the Weeds Explained

36 Then he left the crowds and went into the house. And his disciples came to him, saying, "Explain to us the parable of the weeds of the field." 37 He answered, "The one who sows the good seed is the Son of Man. 38 The field is the world, and the good seed is the sons of the kingdom. The weeds are the sons of the evil one, 39 and the enemy who sowed them is the devil. The harvest is the end of the age, and the reapers are angels. 40 Just as the weeds are gathered and burned with fire, so will it be at the end of the age. 41 The Son of Man will send his angels, and they will gather out of his kingdom all causes of sin and all law-breakers, 42 and throw them into the fiery furnace. In that place there will be weeping and gnashing of teeth. 43 Then the righteous will shine like the sun in the kingdom of their Father. He who has ears, let him hear.

_____

_____

_____

_____

_____

This is a very profound story that depicts the contrast between wickedness and evil and the separation of the two that doesn't happen until the end times. Where are the wicked? They're everywhere, and you can't tell the difference. At the surface, they are amongst you, and you are amongst them. And, it's not your job to pull up the weeds. Why? Because you can't. You are going to have to deal with them. In other words, they're going to be around you all the time. So, what's it going to require? Incredible spiritual discernment. Because you, in essence, on the surface, can't tell. The interesting thing here is He's talking about wheat grains. And when we look at weeds, when we think of weeds, we can tell the difference between weed and plant. No problem. But in this case, the Greek here is that it's a type of grain and they call it weeds, but it's the type of grain that looks the same. And you can't tell the difference other than inside. And the only ones who know the difference are the professionals, so that's why they grew up together. You're not going to know if one's wicked or one's not per se. As you get discernment, you'll know. But your job is to recognize that you're going to grow up with this, and you can't separate yourself to a cloister where there never is wickedness. It's going to be around you all the time. And the enemy, which we'll see, is going to use that.

Word Definitions: **weeds:** kind of darnel, resembling wheat except the grains are black
lawlessness: contempt and violation of law, iniquity, wickedness

How could Christ call Peter, who just previously was recognized the "rock of the church," now equivalent to Satan? What is important to understand about this in our own lives?

Read Matthew 16:21–23:

Jesus Foretells His Death and Resurrection
21 From that time Jesus began to show his disciples that he must go to Jerusalem and suffer many things from the elders and chief priests and scribes, and be killed, and on the third day be raised. 22 And Peter took him aside and began

---

> to rebuke him, saying, "Far be it from you, Lord![a] This shall never happen to you." 23 But he turned and said to Peter, "Get behind me, Satan! You are a hindrance[b] to me. For you are not setting your mind on the things of God, but on the things of man."

_____

_____

_____

_____

_____

Here Christ had called Peter the enemy after a few verses, but before that he was a holy man of God who had this great insight from God. And now he was an offense. On what basis did He call it an offense?

Peter had flipped from understanding the things of God to completely rejecting the things of God. Why? Because the enemy's worked on him to not have a thought of what Christ was saying in any way, but only what he thought on his own. He used his own will, his own ideas, his own plan—all the things of men. Get behind me, Satan. And you're being influenced by the work of Satan, which is a stumbling block because you're drifting back under the influence of Satan and his principalities and powers.

And again, it's around this lack of spiritual power that is being infiltrated, driven by the enemy. So, he's attacking you directly. So, when there's an attack of Satan, it is personal. It's coming against you. You're a believer. And again, it's to destroy you, to thwart what God would be up to, particularly when there is an opportunity for Satan to bring adversity against you and to harm you. Then, you move farther away from God by working on how to solve the problem on your own. Now it's double. You've fallen into his trap as you begin contributing to making your situation worse, and you're going to do a bunch of things that are going to make a bigger hole, a bigger problem, a bigger issue that God would have solved more easily and more quickly. You believe God had the power to come against this, but you never took it. Instead, you turned to what Satan brought. But you never knew how to deal with it because you're responding in the flesh. This is why it's so critical to understand that this is an attack of Satan and only God can help solve it.

LESSON 4:
CAUSES OF ADVERSITY (CONTINUED)

Word Definitions: **stumbling block:** any impediment placed in the way and causing one to stumble or fall, (a stumbling block, occasion of stumbling i.e., a rock which is a cause of stumbling)

things of men: with the added notion of weakness, by which man is led into a mistake or prompted to sin, with the adjunct notion of contempt or disdainful pity

SATAN USES THOSE WHO OPPOSE US.

How does Satan and the demonic use others to draw us away from God and into problems of the world? What exactly happens in these dynamics in our heart? Why?

Read Ephesians 4:25–31:

[25] Therefore, having put away falsehood, let each one of you speak the truth with his neighbor, for we are members one of another. [26] Be angry and do not sin; do not let the sun go down on your anger, [27] and give no opportunity to the devil.[28] Let the thief no longer steal, but rather let him labor, doing honest work with his own hands, so that he may have something to share with anyone in need.[29] Let no corrupting talk come out of your mouths, but only such as is good for building up, as fits the occasion, that it may give grace to those who hear. [30] And do not grieve the Holy Spirit of God, by whom you were sealed for the day of redemption. [31] Let all bitterness and wrath and anger and clamor and slander be put away from you, along with all malice.

_____

_____

_____

_____

_____

The enemy uses self-centered people to get you angry. He'll use whomever he can. Whoever is around you, unbelievers and especially believers, because you don't expect it from them. Anger is not sin. It is perfectly normal and proper to have anger—someone, something has angered you—crossed your line of justice. However, what you do with that anger can turn into sin. We are not to let the devil get a foothold and develop roots of bitterness, unforgiveness, hardness, broken relationships, burdens, etc. that cause us adversity. When this happens, he pulls you out of the Kingdom and you go deeper and deeper and deeper into the world of destruction and now experience more adversity. You let unwholesome talk come out of your mouth. You respond, you react, you go with malice, you go with wrath, you go with all these things, and you grieve the Holy Spirit. Satan's got you because of what he has done. He's used a person or people to come against you in some way. They've wronged you in something. They did something wrong. They didn't show up. They didn't respond. They didn't perform. They said they were going to do something and didn't do it. They've let you down. They hurt you. They speak against you. There are a thousand different things that can happen to you. And, by the way, how often is that going to happen to you? Often! Maybe every day. All the time. Why is it going to happen all the time and for the rest of your life? Because self-centered people are everywhere, and they're not going away. They are everywhere because they are a primary tool of Satan.

Word Definitions: **angry:** to provoke, to arouse to anger, to be provoked to anger, be angry, be wroth
wrath: indignation, exasperation
unwholesome talk: rotten, putrefied, corrupted by one and no longer fit for use, worn out, of poor quality, bad, unfit for use, worthless
grieve: to make sorrowful, to affect with sadness, cause grief, to throw into sorrow, offend
bitterness: bitter gall, extreme wickedness, a bitter root, and so producing a bitter fruit; malice, malignity
malice: ill-will, desire to injure, wickedness, depravity, wickedness that is not ashamed to break laws, evil, trouble

What specifically do people do to attack us? How does this work and why does this work? What causes us problems and why?

> **Read Psalm 7:1–2, 14:**
>
> In You Do I Take Refuge
> A Shiggaion[a] of David, which he sang to the Lord concerning the words of Cush, a Benjaminite.
> **7** O Lord my God, in you do I take refuge;
>   save me from all my pursuers and deliver me,
> ² lest like a lion they tear my soul apart,

> rending it in pieces, with none to deliver.
> [14] Behold, the wicked man conceives evil
> and is pregnant with mischief
> and gives birth to lies.

_____

_____

_____

_____

_____

    This psalm states there will be another attack of Satan by having people coming against us, particularly when they're lying. That's a big one; especially in today's culture where lying is now accepted as a normal way to get what they want. People literally can lie and spin things against you. We know they're speaking a lie, but they're so clever at how they do it, it is most difficult to deal with. We can argue it and debate it, but we must realize who has the power? Satan loves using opposition and using people to oppose us and engage us in conflict.

    To drag us out of the Kingdom into what can be called a low-level grade of infection, Christians are walking around angry. They're frustrated. Nothing's going well, and they are mad all the time, and this thing's always against me, and I can't resolve anything.

Word Definitions: **persecute:** harass

falsehood: deception, disappointment, deception (what deceives or disappoints or betrays one), deceit, fraud, wrong, fraudulently, wrongfully

In this story of Goliath, how does an enemy come against us, and what is a typical response? Why is this a problem? What is the enemy attempting to do? Why?

Read 1 Samuel 17:1–26:

David and Goliath

17 Now the Philistines gathered their armies for battle. And they were gathered at Socoh, which belongs to Judah, and encamped between Socoh and Azekah, in Ephes-dammim. [2] And Saul and the men of Israel were gathered, and encamped in the Valley of Elah, and drew up in line of battle against the

Philistines. ³ And the Philistines stood on the mountain on the one side, and Israel stood on the mountain on the other side, with a valley between them. ⁴ And there came out from the camp of the Philistines a champion named Goliath of Gath, whose height was six[a] cubits[b] and a span. ⁵ He had a helmet of bronze on his head, and he was armed with a coat of mail, and the weight of the coat was five thousand shekels[c] of bronze. ⁶ And he had bronze armor on his legs, and a javelin of bronze slung between his shoulders. ⁷ The shaft of his spear was like a weaver's beam, and his spear's head weighed six hundred shekels of iron. And his shield-bearer went before him. ⁸ He stood and shouted to the ranks of Israel, "Why have you come out to draw up for battle? Am I not a Philistine, and are you not servants of Saul? Choose a man for yourselves, and let him come down to me. ⁹ If he is able to fight with me and kill me, then we will be your servants. But if I prevail against him and kill him, then you shall be our servants and serve us." ¹⁰ And the Philistine said, "I defy the ranks of Israel this day. Give me a man, that we may fight together." ¹¹ When Saul and all Israel heard these words of the Philistine, they were dismayed and greatly afraid.

¹² Now David was the son of an Ephrathite of Bethlehem in Judah, named Jesse, who had eight sons. In the days of Saul the man was already old and advanced in years.[d] ¹³ The three oldest sons of Jesse had followed Saul to the battle. And the names of his three sons who went to the battle were Eliab the firstborn, and next to him Abinadab, and the third Shammah. ¹⁴ David was the youngest. The three eldest followed Saul, 15 but David went back and forth from Saul to feed his father's sheep at Bethlehem. ¹⁶ For forty days the Philistine came forward and took his stand, morning and evening.

¹⁷ And Jesse said to David his son, "Take for your brothers an ephah[e] of this parched grain, and these ten loaves, and carry them quickly to the camp to your brothers. ¹⁸ Also take these ten cheeses to the commander of their thousand. See if your brothers are well, and bring some token from them."

¹⁹ Now Saul and they and all the men of Israel were in the Valley of Elah, fighting with the Philistines. ²⁰ And David rose early in the morning and left the sheep with a keeper and took the provisions and went, as Jesse had commanded him. And he came to the encampment as the host was going out to the battle line, shouting the war cry. ²¹ And Israel and the Philistines drew up for battle, army against army. ²² And David left the things in charge of the keeper of the baggage and ran to the ranks and went and greeted his brothers. ²³ As he talked with them, behold, the champion, the Philistine of Gath, Goliath by

> name, came up out of the ranks of the Philistines and spoke the same words as before. And David heard him.
>
> [24] All the men of Israel, when they saw the man, fled from him and were much afraid. [25] And the men of Israel said, "Have you seen this man who has come up? Surely he has come up to defy Israel. And the king will enrich the man who kills him with great riches and will give him his daughter and make his father's house free in Israel." [26] And David said to the men who stood by him, "What shall be done for the man who kills this Philistine and takes away the reproach from Israel? For who is this uncircumcised Philistine, that he should defy the armies of the living God?"

_____

_____

_____

_____

_____

Here's a picture of Satan using a person who basically says, "I defy you. And you want to fight me, go ahead." The enemy is using this person "to come against you and I know I'm coming against you and the power of God. In essence, let's see what you got." And Saul, who had access to God, responded how? With great dismay and fear. Because in his mind they were bigger and more powerful. He was still trying to fight it in the flesh instead of thinking about what God had promised.

Remember, we often feel we are going against Goliath, that there is no way we can win.

This can happen in business, in ministry, in our family, anywhere we feel there is someone who has power over you. Our conclusion, then, thinking in the natural, is that there is no way we're going to get through this. The second we go into fear and dismay, the enemy has successfully found a way to use somebody against you, to carry you to fear.

Word Definitions: **prevail:** overcome, endure, have power, be able
greatly afraid: exceedingly be fearful, be dreadful
dismayed: to be shattered, be dismayed, be scared
fight: to engage in battle, wage war
defy: to reproach, taunt, blaspheme, jeopardize, rail, upbraid

LESSON 5:
HOW DO I KNOW WHICH ADVERSITY I AM FACING?
HOW DO I OVERCOME THESE ADVERSITIES?

"If we have been invited to repent but have not, then the adversity is becoming more pronounced."

Usually, we know right away what adversity we are facing especially when we are walking in the Spirit. If we don't know, we are not to second guess, but just proceed according to the wisdom we are receiving as to how the Lord wants to deal with this adversity. Pray through it and respond to God's instructions.

ABIDING, WALKING IN THE SPIRIT:

1. **Is this general adversity?** Is this a simple frustration that is not against me personally, but comes because I live in a world controlled by Satan, a world of steal, kill, and destroy, a world of entropy that is falling apart and filled with self-centered people? It should not surprise me, and normally my days will experience frustration and things that do not work perfectly as the things I own and have will break down.

2. **Is this a test of faith?** We will know if we have been receiving Rhema Words from God—promises, prophetic foretelling or forth-telling, truths of transformation, deliverance, etc. As we are abiding in Him, we know what we are being tested on, and thus, are to cooperate with the test and let Him complete our faith and overcome this adversity through this test of faith.

3. **Is this pruning?** Are we tired, weary, not enjoying our work, our marriage, our family, or our ministry? Then something is wrong, and this adversity is meant to get our attention to allow God to cut back our activities, so we can regain margin and sweetness in our life. We are to fully cooperate.

4. **Is this coming from selfishness?** If we are not abiding in the Vine, in His Word, hearing His voice, or have gone to the flesh through self-determination of selfish, sinful thoughts, then by definition we are walking in the flesh (carnal). Romans 8:5–8 says that when we live in the flesh, we put to death the life of the Spirit in us (as if no effect), are at enmity against God (working against the will of God), and cannot please God (not enjoying God's life and purposes in and for us). In essence then, our adversities will be coming from selfishness. We have left the Kingdom of God because we are exercising our will

and not surrendering to the King and His will, and thus have lost our peace, joy, freedom, and perhaps gone to unforgiveness—all indicators that we are not walking in the Spirit, in the Kingdom. We are to repent immediately and return to the relationship of the Spirit and the power of the Kingdom, where God can take authority against this adversity.

5. If we have been invited to repent but have not, then the adversity is becoming more pronounced. **Is it then coming from being disciplined?** The Father wants us to experience the severity of the adversity, so our response will be to repent and decide to return to the relationship of the Spirit and the power of the Kingdom, where God can take authority against this adversity.

6. The adversity has gotten worse, and if we have been invited to repent once again, but have not, then **is this coming from being led into judgment?** The adversity is now leading to even more severe consequences of my life, so we repent and decide to return to the relationship of the Spirit and the power of the Kingdom, where God can take authority against this adversity.

7. **Is this coming from a direct attack from Satan who is coming against me to thwart God's will in my life and cause me to cease following God, thereby taking things back into his own hands?** If so, we are to stand against it so God can take authority against this adversity.

HOW TO OVERCOME ADVERSITY:

THE FIRST PRINCIPLE IS WALKING WITH GOD IN ALL THINGS.
What does Christ say is key to following Him as we seek solutions to adversity? Why is this so critical to the process? Why might it be so difficult?

Read Matthew 10:34–39; 16:24–27:

Not Peace, but a Sword

[34] "Do not think that I have come to bring peace to the earth. I have not come to bring peace, but a sword. [35] For I have come to set a man against his father, and a daughter against her mother, and a daughter-in-law against her mother-in-law. [36] And a person's enemies will be those of his own household. [37] Whoever loves father or mother more than me is not worthy of me, and whoever loves son or daughter more than me is not worthy of me. [38] And whoever does not take his cross and follow me is not worthy of me. [39] Whoever finds his life will lose it, and whoever loses his life for my sake will find it.

LESSON 5:
HOW DO I KNOW WHICH ADVERSITY I AM FACING?
HOW DO I OVERCOME THESE ADVERSITIES?

> Take Up Your Cross and Follow Jesus
>
> [24] Then Jesus told his disciples, "If anyone would come after me, let him deny himself and take up his cross and follow me. [25] For whoever would save his life[a] will lose it, but whoever loses his life for my sake will find it. [26] For what will it profit a man if he gains the whole world and forfeits his soul? Or what shall a man give in return for his soul? [27] For the Son of Man is going to come with his angels in the glory of his Father, and then he will repay each person according to what he has done.

_____

_____

_____

_____

_____

Jesus lays out clearly this key principle in our choice that is required for Him to act, to work to resolve our adversities; He must be first and preeminent in all things all the time.

As you're seeking the answer to the adversity, you have to come to Him first. Walk with Him first. Seek Him first. He said that He has the answer. And it's more important to come to Him first, rather than trying to please somebody else. Don't let pleasing somebody else get in the way. Come to Him first. Come to Him first and learn to process with Him. It is straightforward. He has the answers, so we need to come to Him for the answers.

To fulfill this, we go to Matthew 16 where we read, "We are to deny self." Take up the cross and follow Him. That's the key to avoiding further adversity – do not attempt to figure this out on your own but deny self. The answer is not you. Keep thinking that the answer is Him. Why? Because He knows all answers. He's above all things. He can make things happen. You have a problem. He can resolve it. He can change it. And it's not naturally changing. He's not giving you the wisdom to maneuver around it and come up with a great solution. He's going to fix it supernaturally. He can do things that you can't do. So why don't you just come to Him?

The first principle is: Come to Him, first and foremost.

Word Definitions:

above: over, beyond, more than

worthy: value, worth

follow: to follow one who precedes, join him as his attendant, accompany him, to join one as a disciple, become or be his disciple

deny: to forget one's self, lose sight of one's self and one's own interests

As we seek Him individually, what next is important in the process? Why is this so critical to seeking His answers? What is the benefit to us?

Read Luke 11:14–23:

Jesus and Beelzebul

[14] Now he was casting out a demon that was mute. When the demon had gone out, the mute man spoke, and the people marveled. [15] But some of them said, "He casts out demons by Beelzebul, the prince of demons," [16] while others, to test him, kept seeking from him a sign from heaven. [17] But he, knowing their thoughts, said to them, "Every kingdom divided against itself is laid waste, and a divided household falls. [18] And if Satan also is divided against himself, how will his kingdom stand? For you say that I cast out demons by Beelzebul. [19] And if I cast out demons by Beelzebul, by whom do your sons cast them out? Therefore they will be your judges. [20] But if it is by the finger of God that I cast out demons, then the kingdom of God has come upon you. [21] When a strong man, fully armed, guards his own palace, his goods are safe; [22] but when one stronger than he attacks him and overcomes him, he takes away his armor in which he trusted and divides his spoil. 23 Whoever is not with me is against me, and whoever does not gather with me scatters.

_____

_____

_____

_____

_____

He tells us the next part of the process—once we individually have a clear understanding that we are to go to Him first and foremost—then we need to seek unity with our spouse, friend, or group to confirm God's will—His answer to your issue, your problem, your adversity. Go to unity, seek His will together, and then come to unity about what He says about this adversity. It's okay to disagree, but keep processing, processing, processing until you get to unity because that's where the power will be. And you must hear what He has to say. The first principle is to come to Him, get His answer, and your answer will come in unity, in confirmation, as you process with another who also has come to Him.

Word Definitions: **to be divided:** into opposing parts, to be at variance, in dissension
falls: to be cast down from a state of prosperity, to fall from a state of uprightness, to perish, (i.e., come to an end, disappear, cease)
stand: to cause or make to stand, to place, put, set
stronger: strong, violent, forcibly uttered, firm, sure

Now, let's look at the specific responses in order to have God resolve these different adversities that we face. Since they are from different sources, the responses are not all the same, but related to the source:

1.   GENERAL ADVERSITY:

Stay in Peace, in the Kingdom:
To respond, what is important to properly process the solution to general adversity?

Read Romans 14:17:

[17] For the kingdom of God is not a matter of eating and drinking but of righteousness and peace and joy in the Holy Spirit.

_____

_____

_____

_____

_____

LESSON 5:
HOW DO I KNOW WHICH ADVERSITY I AM FACING?
HOW DO I OVERCOME THESE ADVERSITIES?

The first thing is to stay in peace. The Kingdom of God is to stay in the Kingdom. It's not a surprise. I'm not going to get distracted out of the Kingdom. I'm not going to get upset about this. Doesn't surprise me, it's general adversity. I'm going to stay in the Kingdom, and thus stay in peace and joy. This is not going to draw me out into the flesh, since the solution will be given here by the King in the Kingdom.

Word Definitions: **righteousness:** integrity, virtue, purity of life, rightness, correctness of thinking, feeling, and acting

peace: shalom

joy: gladness, joy received from you

What does Christ promise as we experience trouble? What does this look like for me?

> **Read John 16:33:**
>
> 33 I have said these things to you, that in me you may have peace. In the world you will have tribulation. But take heart; I have overcome the world."

_____

_____

_____

_____

Jesus states that He told us that in the world we are going to have general adversity, so that we may understand that the key is for us in the middle of this general adversity to have (remain in) peace in Christ. In Christ you have peace. Stay in peace. The world is going to produce trouble for us but stay in peace. Stay in Shalom. Don't let the enemy steal your peace.

Word Definitions: **peace:** shalom

trouble: pressing, pressing together, pressure, oppression, affliction, tribulation, distress, straits

courage: good cheer

overcome: conquer, to carry off the victory, come off victorious, of Christ, victorious over all His foes

Despite the trouble we encounter, what does God promise? What does this mean to us? How do we react to this?

Read Romans 8:28:

28 And we know that for those who love God all things work together for good,[a] for those who are called according to his purpose.

_____

_____

_____

_____

_____

Remember all things work together for our good, our best, our resolution of our adversities. He can make this adversity work for your good. This general adversity is affecting you, but He will give you a way for this to be made good. Do not fret and walk with Him into the good solution. It will be unique to you. It affected you generally since it was affecting all people around you, but He'll give you a way for it to be made good for you as you seek Him to make it good for you uniquely. It will be resolved. Stay in peace and look to Him to resolve this, and it will be.

Word Definition: **good:** useful, salutary, pleasant, agreeable, joyful, happy, excellent, distinguished, upright, honorable

Seek Wisdom:

Then, what are we to seek as we need answers to our adversity? What does God promise? What does this mean to us?

Read James 1:5–8:

5 If any of you lacks wisdom, let him ask God, who gives generously to all without reproach, and it will be given him. 6 But let him ask in faith, with no doubting, for the one who doubts is like a wave of the sea that is driven and tossed by the wind. 7 For that person must not suppose that he will receive anything from the Lord; 8 he is a double-minded man, unstable in all his ways.

_____

_____

_____

_____

_____

We need to know what to do in this general adversity for it to be resolved. Go to God and ask: What do you have to say? How would you have us deal with this? What are you going to do? We need wisdom. Do not get led out of the Kingdom and make a mess of things. Stay in your peace and then receive the wisdom that God promises to give the solution to this issue.

Word Definitions: **ask:** beg, call for, crave, desire, require
liberally: simply, openly, frankly, sincerely
faith: conviction of the truth of anything, belief
doubting: to oppose, strive with dispute, contend

Listen/Follow:

As we ask for wisdom, what is our role? What will He speak, and how specific will it be? Why is this important to us?

Read Isaiah 30:18–22:

The Lord Will Be Gracious

[18] Therefore the Lord waits to be gracious to you,
   and therefore he exalts himself to show mercy to you.
For the Lord is a God of justice;
   blessed are all those who wait for him.
[19] For a people shall dwell in Zion, in Jerusalem; you shall weep no more. He will surely be gracious to you at the sound of your cry. As soon as he hears it, he answers you. [20] And though the Lord give you the bread of adversity and the water of affliction, yet your Teacher will not hide himself anymore, but your eyes shall see your Teacher. [21] And your ears shall hear a word behind you, saying, "This is the way, walk in it," when you turn to the right or when you turn to the left. [22] Then you will defile your carved idols overlaid with silver and your gold-plated metal images. You will scatter them as unclean things. You will say to them, "Be gone!"

LESSON 5:
HOW DO I KNOW WHICH ADVERSITY I AM FACING?
HOW DO I OVERCOME THESE ADVERSITIES?

_____

_____

_____

_____

_____

He states, "I give you the wisdom, follow exactly what I tell you to do. Stay in your peace and expect this to be resolved. You are passing through it. Now receive My wisdom as I give you what you are to do and what I will do to bring resolution to this general adversity that you are facing."

Word Definitions: **hear/listen**: listen to, obey, to hear (perceive by ear), to hear of or concerning, hear (have power to hear), to hear with attention or interest, listen to, to understand

Passes Quickly/Frustration over:
What does He say He will give us, and what should we expect? What does this mean to us about this problem?

> **Read John 14:27:**
>
> [27] Peace I leave with you; my peace I give to you. Not as the world gives do I give to you. Let not your hearts be troubled, neither let them be afraid.

_____

_____

_____

_____

Christ states that He is giving us peace. His peace—not as the world gives it (based upon the circumstances). He's giving you this ability to see what He understands. He wants you to understand that this general adversity is going to pass. It is not really going to affect you greatly. Or, here's what He's going to show you about it so you can stay in your peace and understand the resolution. Or, if there's going to be an impact, he'll show you what it looks like and what its impact and the resolution will be. Thus, stay in and receive the peace that Christ gives—it is spiritual.

LESSON 5:
HOW DO I KNOW WHICH ADVERSITY I AM FACING?
HOW DO I OVERCOME THESE ADVERSITIES?

Word Definitions:

peace: shalom

give: to give something to someone; of one's own accord to give one something, to his advantage, to bestow a gift, to grant, give to one asking, let have, to supply, furnish, necessary things

Do not let it steal your peace or joy:

How do we handle this adversity? What is important to get through this?

Read and practice Isaiah 26:3–4:

³ You keep him in perfect peace
   whose mind is stayed on you,
   because he trusts in you.
⁴ Trust in the Lord forever,
   for the Lord God is an everlasting rock.

He gives us two key practices to receive and maintain peace:

1. You will keep Him in perfect peace, as we keep our mind on God.

2. Trust in God. The resolution will come and thus, you can trust it.

So, keep your mind on Him, not on the problem. If you do, your heart will stay in perfect peace. The word here for perfect peace is shalom. Peace. You'll keep getting more shalom as you stay in shalom. It's a general adversity and you will get through it. You haven't lost your peace, and you will see the resolution of it.

LESSON 5:
HOW DO I KNOW WHICH ADVERSITY I AM FACING?
HOW DO I OVERCOME THESE ADVERSITIES?

Word Definitions: **keep:** to guard, watch, watch over, to preserve, guard from dangers, observe, guard with fidelity, keep secret

mind: purpose, imagination, device (intellectual framework)

stayed: to lean, lay, rest, support, put, uphold, lean upon

perfect peace: shalom

to ordain: establish

2.   TEST OF FAITH:

We have the Spirit through the New Covenant:
What does God promise us as we go through a test of faith? Why is this so wonderful for those of us who struggle with faith? How does it work practically?

Read Jeremiah 31:31–34:

The New Covenant

31 "Behold, the days are coming, declares the Lord, when I will make a new covenant with the house of Israel and the house of Judah, **32** not like the covenant that I made with their fathers on the day when I took them by the hand to bring them out of the land of Egypt, my covenant that they broke, though I was their husband, declares the Lord. **33** For this is the covenant that I will make with the house of Israel after those days, declares the Lord: I will put my law within them, and I will write it on their hearts. And I will be their God, and they shall be my people. **34** And no longer shall each one teach his neighbor and each his brother, saying, 'Know the Lord,' for they shall all know me, from the least of them to the greatest, declares the Lord. For I will forgive their iniquity, and I will remember their sin no more."

_____

_____

_____

_____

God has spoken through the Covenant: I'm going to bless you to make you a blessing. I'm going to fulfill what I said. I will fulfill my side of the agreement. (The Covenant is an agreement between us and God.) We need to fulfill our side of the agreement, and God will work His side of the deal. He will give us the faith to believe what He speaks. It's His work, not yours. The Holy Spirit is within us to give us faith.

Word Definitions: **write:** record, enroll, inscribe, engrave, write in, write on, to write down, describe in writing, to register, to decree

hearts: inner man, mind, will, understanding, inner part, midst, midst (of things), heart (of man), soul, heart (of man), knowledge, thinking, reflection, memory, inclination, resolution, determination (of will)

inward parts: midst, among, inner part, middle, inward part, physical sense, as seat of thought and emotion, as faculty of thought and emotion

Secret Revelation:

What does God promise to give us as we seek to understand faith and what He is speaking to us? Why is this so important to us?

Read Luke 10:21–24:

Jesus Rejoices in the Father's Will

21 In that same hour he rejoiced in the Holy Spirit and said, "I thank you, Father, Lord of heaven and earth, that you have hidden these things from the wise and understanding and revealed them to little children; yes, Father, for such was your gracious will.[a] 22 All things have been handed over to me by my Father, and no one knows who the Son is except the Father, or who the Father is except the Son and anyone to whom the Son chooses to reveal him." 23 Then turning to the disciples he said privately, "Blessed are the eyes that see what you see! 24 For I tell you that many prophets and kings desired to see what you see, and did not see it, and to hear what you hear, and did not hear it."

_____

_____

_____

_____

_____

This involves the spiritual—not the natural—secret revelation that is received spiritually and not naturally. There'll be more revelation given to you when you're seeking in the Kingdom. And He said your approach to the Kingdom should be like that of a little child. Let your natural curiosity carry you farther to receive this secret revelation, the parts you might not understand. What else does God have to say to you? Could God help you understand why you're struggling with this? What else can God reveal to us that will help us receive His truth, His words, His depth? When a child asks a question, what do they expect? They expect the answer. They don't think: I must not be sophisticated enough to get your super profound answer because I'm just not good enough. I'll ask it, but I don't ever expect an answer. What do they do? They just ask the question. The same is true for us. If we don't answer, they keep asking and they keep asking, saying, "I don't quite understand that. Help me understand in a different way." God says He will reveal to you His secret, spiritual answer.

He says, "Blessed are you who have that privilege." Why don't we take that privilege? We are seeking depth of the answer. We are to have the heart of a child who says, I expect you to answer me and will stay with it until you do.

Word Definition: **revealed:** uncover, lay open what has been veiled or covered up, disclose, make bare; to make known, make manifest, disclose what before was unknown

Believe that what He has spoken – His words (Rhema) will come to pass:
What is critical for us to believe about what Christ has authored? Why is this so important to our process?

Read Joshua 21:43–45:

[43] Thus the Lord gave to Israel all the land that he swore to give to their fathers. And they took possession of it, and they settled there. [44] And the Lord gave them rest on every side just as he had sworn to their fathers. Not one of all their enemies had withstood them, for the Lord had given all their enemies into their hands. [45] Not one word of all the good promises that the Lord had made to the house of Israel had failed; all came to pass.

LESSON 5:
HOW DO I KNOW WHICH ADVERSITY I AM FACING?
HOW DO I OVERCOME THESE ADVERSITIES?

_____

_____

_____

_____

_____

Not one word of all the good promises that the Lord made to the House of Israel failed. All came to pass. Every single word of the promise came to pass. What God said happened. We must expect it to come to pass.

It is okay to be struggling with that but ask God to help you receive certainty that what He said is true even if the circumstances are tough to accept. We must always stand on the truth that what God says will come to pass; we cannot move away from that.

Word Definition: **to come to pass**: happened as spoken, fulfilled

Go to the throne room with boldness.
What is our great privilege in this process? On what basis is this privilege, and what does God tell us about this privilege? Why is it so critical to us personally and to our struggle with faith?

Read Hebrews 10:19–25, 35–38:

The Full Assurance of Faith
[19] Therefore, brothers,[a] since we have confidence to enter the holy places by the blood of Jesus, [20] by the new and living way that he opened for us through the curtain, that is, through his flesh, [21] and since we have a great priest over the house of God, [22] let us draw near with a true heart in full assurance of faith, with our hearts sprinkled clean from an evil conscience and our bodies washed with pure water. [23] Let us hold fast the confession of our hope without wavering, for he who promised is faithful. [24] And let us consider how to stir up one another to love and good works, [25] not neglecting to meet together, as is the habit of some, but encouraging one another, and all the more as you see the Day drawing near.

> 35 Therefore do not throw away your confidence, which has a great
> reward.36 For you have need of endurance, so that when you have done the will
> of God you may receive what is promised. 37 For,
> "Yet a little while,
>   and the coming one will come and will not delay;
> 38 but my righteous one shall live by faith,
>   and if he shrinks back,
> my soul has no pleasure in him."

_____

_____

_____

_____

_____

As we are struggling with our faith, we are to go to Him with boldness. Where? The throne room, where we're seated with Christ at the right hand of the Father and where we are to start talking about the struggle. He says you have the privilege because Christ has released the separation and given you the privilege through the tearing of the veil: a picture of what happened in the temple at His death/resurrection. The temple was set up with a demarcation where there was a court of Gentiles: a court of women, a court of men, a court of the priest, and then there was a Holy of Holies. Here the only one who could go in was the high priest. And there was a curtain (veil) 80 feet high. And he's the only one who could go in once a year to have atonement and talk to God and provide atonement for the nation.

First, he sacrificed for himself, then for his family, then for the entire nation of God. And because he was the only one who could go in and there's only one high priest, they actually draped a rope around his ankle in case he died in there so they could pull him out. When Christ died on the cross, He said: It is finished. The full and complete atonement for all of mankind's sin was finished/complete. At that moment, the curtain tore from top to bottom and thus opened up the privilege that is now available to everybody who has received this atonement personally (believed Christ as Savior and accepted Him into their heart—born again). Everyone can now go directly into the Holy of Holies, go into the throne room.

So, because of this privilege, with boldness and confidence, start talking to God. He tells us to go in with a sincere heart. In the Greek, the word is authentic heart. If you're struggling with faith, what do you want to talk about? We can be honest and admit that we are struggling to believe that everything God said would happen. Ask God to tell us more so that we might understand it better. Ask for more hope. Ask for a signal for good. He will be happy to share with us more and give us more secret revelation.

Remember: Do not throw away this privilege of coming to God with confidence and boldness as you will be richly rewarded. You need to persevere so that when you've done the will of God, you will receive what He has promised. Let your burden be His burden. Don't throw away the privilege He's giving you. He will reward you for that. It will greatly benefit you, so please come and take advantage of this wonderful privilege.

Word Definition: **boldness:** freedom in speaking, unreservedness in speech, openly, frankly, (i.e., without concealment, without ambiguity or circumlocution, without the use of figures and comparisons), free and fearless confidence, cheerful courage, boldness, assurance
reward: payment of wages due, recompence
endurance: steadfastness, constancy

What does He remind us about His role in faith? Why is this so important to us and how does this practically work for us?

Read Hebrews 12:1–2:

Jesus, Founder and Perfecter of Our Faith
12 Therefore, since we are surrounded by so great a cloud of witnesses, let us also lay aside every weight, and sin which clings so closely, and let us run with endurance the race that is set before us, ² looking to Jesus, the founder and perfecter of our faith, who for the joy that was set before him endured the cross, despising the shame, and is seated at the right hand of the throne of God.

_____

_____

_____

_____

_____

He says to remember: I'm the author and finisher of faith. It's my work. It's my work. It's my work, not yours. Quit wondering what's wrong with you. Nothing. Thank goodness. He said the only reason you're not getting it is really simple. You are not sticking with Him. You're not coming to receive His work. You're trying to figure out everything yourself, and you're not coming to be with Him; or you just keep waiting for it, and then it never happens. And then you lose your hope, and you lose the ability to receive what He is prepared to do and give. So, stay with it.

Word Definitions: **author:** one that takes the lead in anything and thus affords an example, a predecessor in a matter, pioneer

finisher: a perfector, one who has in his own person raised faith to its perfection and so set before us the highest example of faith

In this story of David, how did he get to faith, and what truths did he come to? Why is this so important for us and our process of coming to faith?

> **Read 2 Samuel 7:27–29:**
>
> [27] For you, O Lord of hosts, the God of Israel, have made this revelation to your servant, saying, 'I will build you a house.' Therefore your servant has found courage to pray this prayer to you. [28] And now, O Lord God, you are God, and your words are true, and you have promised this good thing to your servant. [29] Now therefore may it please you to bless the house of your servant, so that it may continue forever before you. For you, O Lord God, have spoken, and with your blessing shall the house of your servant be blessed forever."

_____

_____

_____

_____

_____

This is a scenario where David had said: I think it's a good idea to build God a permanent temple in Jerusalem because they only had the tabernacle, which they were carrying from place to place. And Nathan, who was God's confirming prophet said: That's a good idea. Go ahead.

But God goes to Nathan and says, "Come here, son, you forgot a step. You did not ask Me." Nathan apologizes but then asks what God would have said. God says He would not have agreed to it. David is a man of war and cannot build Him a temple. That's not His will. His son can build Him a temple, but not David. Instead, God gives David the promise that through His line, his lineage, He will bring the Messiah. I'm going to bring Jesus Christ through him. Tell that to David. That's the promise I give to him.

Nathan gives that promise to David. So, David goes and says: I found courage in my heart to pray this prayer: "What are you talking about? What exactly does that mean? I don't understand what that means. I've heard the promise, but I don't understand it." He found courage in his heart to go to the throne room and ask for more information. And he prays, and he prays, and he prays because he needed to understand what God said and what it meant. How would this happen? And so, he prays and prays and prays until he gets to verse 28: "And now I know these three things: You are God. I'm not. And you can fulfill all. You're the great I am. You can fulfill what you just said. Your words are true and absolute, and they will come to pass. And then: You've applied this promise to me personally. I receive this fully—it applies to me personally—not generically but is a promise to me.

And then once these questions move fully toward faith, David moves to verse 29 where He says: Go ahead and do it. So be it. Fulfill it. Now that I have faith, I now believe it, and I expect it to happen, so I can now pray: May it please You to fulfill what you have said. Amen, so be it.

This is how it works as we pray it through. Do we understand that this promise is our personal promise? Do we believe God can do it? Do we believe God has the capability of fulfilling that promise? His words apply to us personally in every situation. We can say, "So be it." And you stay with Him in the throne room until you get there. It doesn't matter how long it takes. Stay with Him, and He will give us secrets. He will share His wisdom. He'll give us understanding. Find courage in your heart, boldness in your heart. Do not waste the privilege.

Word Definitions:

revealed: uncover, discover

Jehovah: "the existing One"

to occur: come to pass, be done, be brought about, be finished

word: speaking, thing, speech, saying, utterance

truth: sureness, reliability, stability, continuance, faithfulness

promise: speak, declare, command

good: pleasant, agreeable (to the senses), pleasant (to the higher nature), excellent (of its kind), rich, valuable in estimation, glad, happy, prosperous (of man's sensuous nature), a good thing, benefit, welfare, prosperity, happiness, bounty

pleased: to resolve, be pleased, be determined

What are the truths that you take from this story about how Jehoshaphat dealt with his adversity and went to faith? What is important to you personally?

Read 2 Chronicles 20:1–30:

Jehoshaphat's Prayer

20 After this the Moabites and Ammonites, and with them some of the Meunites,[a] came against Jehoshaphat for battle. 2 Some men came and told Jehoshaphat, "A great multitude is coming against you from Edom,[b] from beyond the sea; and, behold, they are in Hazazon-tamar" (that is, Engedi).3 Then Jehoshaphat was afraid and set his face to seek the Lord, and proclaimed a fast throughout all Judah. 4 And Judah assembled to seek help from the Lord; from all the cities of Judah they came to seek the Lord.

5 And Jehoshaphat stood in the assembly of Judah and Jerusalem, in the house of the Lord, before the new court, 6 and said, "O Lord, God of our fathers, are you not God in heaven? You rule over all the kingdoms of the nations. In your hand are power and might, so that none is able to withstand you. 7 Did you not, our God, drive out the inhabitants of this land before your people Israel, and give it forever to the descendants of Abraham your friend? 8 And they have lived in it and have built for you in it a sanctuary for your name, saying, 9 'If disaster comes upon us, the sword, judgment,[c] or pestilence, or famine, we will stand before this house and before you—for your name is in this house—and cry out to you in our affliction, and you will hear and save.' 10 And now behold, the men of Ammon and Moab and Mount Seir, whom you would not let Israel invade when they came from the land of Egypt, and whom they avoided and did not destroy— 11 behold, they reward us by coming to drive us out of your possession, which you have given us to inherit. 12 O our God, will you not execute judgment on them? For we are powerless against this great horde that is coming against us. We do not know what to do, but our eyes are on you." 13 Meanwhile all Judah stood before the Lord, with their little ones, their wives, and their children. 14 And the Spirit of the Lord came[d] upon Jahaziel the son of Zechariah, son of Benaiah, son of Jeiel, son of Mattaniah, a Levite of the sons of Asaph, in the midst of the assembly. 15 And he said, "Listen, all Judah and inhabitants of Jerusalem and King Jehoshaphat: Thus says the Lord to you, 'Do not be afraid and do not be dismayed at this great horde, for the battle is not yours but God's. 16 Tomorrow go down against them. Behold, they will come up by the ascent of Ziz. You will find them at the end of the valley, east of the wilderness of Jeruel. 17 You will not need to fight in this battle. Stand firm, hold

your position, and see the salvation of the Lord on your behalf, O Judah and Jerusalem.' Do not be afraid and do not be dismayed. Tomorrow go out against them, and the Lord will be with you."

18 Then Jehoshaphat bowed his head with his face to the ground, and all Judah and the inhabitants of Jerusalem fell down before the Lord, worshiping the Lord. 19 And the Levites, of the Kohathites and the Korahites, stood up to praise the Lord, the God of Israel, with a very loud voice.

20 And they rose early in the morning and went out into the wilderness of Tekoa. And when they went out, Jehoshaphat stood and said, "Hear me, Judah and inhabitants of Jerusalem! Believe in the Lord your God, and you will be established; believe his prophets, and you will succeed." 21 And when he had taken counsel with the people, he appointed those who were to sing to the Lord and praise him in holy attire, as they went before the army, and say, "Give thanks to the Lord,
 for his steadfast love endures forever."
22 And when they began to sing and praise, the Lord set an ambush against the men of Ammon, Moab, and Mount Seir, who had come against Judah, so that they were routed. 23 For the men of Ammon and Moab rose against the inhabitants of Mount Seir, devoting them to destruction, and when they had made an end of the inhabitants of Seir, they all helped to destroy one another.

The Lord Delivers Judah
24 When Judah came to the watchtower of the wilderness, they looked toward the horde, and behold, there[e] were dead bodies lying on the ground; none had escaped. 25 When Jehoshaphat and his people came to take their spoil, they found among them, in great numbers, goods, clothing, and precious things, which they took for themselves until they could carry no more. They were three days in taking the spoil, it was so much. 26 On the fourth day they assembled in the Valley of Beracah,[f] for there they blessed the Lord. Therefore the name of that place has been called the Valley of Beracah to this day. 27 Then they returned, every man of Judah and Jerusalem, and Jehoshaphat at their head, returning to Jerusalem with joy, for the Lord had made them rejoice over their enemies. 28 They came to Jerusalem with harps and lyres and trumpets, to the house of the Lord. 29 And the fear of God came on all the kingdoms of the countries when they heard that the Lord had fought against the enemies of Israel. 30 So the realm of Jehoshaphat was quiet, for his God gave him rest all around.

LESSON 5:
HOW DO I KNOW WHICH ADVERSITY I AM FACING?
HOW DO I OVERCOME THESE ADVERSITIES?

_____

_____

_____

_____

_____

We have this great example of Jehoshaphat: He was surrounded by several nations that were far bigger and stronger than he and his nation of Israel. There was no way that he could win and was going to be defeated based on the circumstances. He goes to God and says: Father, we literally do not know what to do. But, because he was understanding the Word, he went back to a promise that says if the nation is living in the Covenant, Israel will not be defeated. He goes back to that promise and basically says to God, "Does that apply to us? We have no idea what to do."

We are not to make the mistake of just applying the generic word by saying or thinking simply that God is going to take care of us. So instead, we pray generically that God takes care of us. But this is not faith and why we receive no resolution. This is what leads to our discouragement and hopelessness.

But Jehoshaphat says, "But our eyes are on you." Their eyes weren't on all the things that were going to come against them or the overwhelming circumstances. They put their eyes on Him, looking for His answer, which He promised to give (authors and finishes faith). God said it was not their battle, but His. He would defeat them. He would fight this battle.

Then, we ask the next question: What now? Specifically, what do You want us to do here? He reminds us that it's His battle, not ours. Tomorrow you go to this specific spot and arm up as if you're going to battle and then you watch what I'm about ready to do. And you've got to believe that what I'm about ready to do will happen. And your demonstration of this faith is that you are going to prepare for battle as if you are actually going to go to battle.

They were told to put the singers out in front, worship, believe, and watch. Then the enemy turned on themselves, and they fought each other and killed each other. It tells us that praise and worship are an important part of this.

Jehoshaphat fully believed, and the people of the nation fully believed. They armed up the next day and got to the designated spot. Jehoshaphat said: If we believe the Word, the promise that God gave Israel, which we've received personally and know what to do, and then believe in the promise, God will fulfill that promise and bring us to victory right before our eyes. Indeed, it was done. There was so much spoil, it took them three days to carry it back. Why did the enemy bring all that stuff with them? They believed that there was no way Israel could beat them. They expected to win and then to occupy Jerusalem—and this is the reason they brought all their belongings with them. God gave their possessions to Jehoshaphat and his people. Today, this promise applies to all of us. Do you believe it? Do you have faith and understand? Do you recognize this promise? Then prepare yourself to see what happens, see what God has planned.

Word Definitions: **seek:** to resort, to seek with care, enquire, require

gathered together: in unity

ask: request help

stand: take one's stand, be in a standing attitude, stand forth, take a stand, present oneself, attend upon, be or become a servant of

believe: be established – same Hebrew words – believe and will be able to believe

prosper: advance, make progress, succeed, be profitable

LESSON 6:
OVERCOMING ADVERSITIES (CONTINUED)

Let's look at our response to God's work in our lives regarding pruning and some of the adversity that we might be experiencing because we are not responding to that pruning.

PRUNING

Fully cooperate with the Father when He is asking you to open up space and margin, and release burdens to live a life of freedom. What has to be cut back (especially what we may consider to be good things but are not God's things right now) to create fruit, more fruit, much fruit?

Look again at the roles of each of Jesus' spiritual analogies as related to the vineyard, vine, the grapes, and wine making:

> **Read John 15:1–5:**
>
> I Am the True Vine
>
> **15** "I am the true vine, and my Father is the vinedresser. [2] Every branch in me that does not bear fruit he takes away, and every branch that does bear fruit he prunes, that it may bear more fruit. [3] Already you are clean because of the word that I have spoken to you. [4] Abide in me, and I in you. As the branch cannot bear fruit by itself, unless it abides in the vine, neither can you, unless you abide in me.[5] I am the vine; you are the branches. Whoever abides in me and I in him, he it is that bears much fruit, for apart from me you can do nothing.

"The vinedresser is the one who has the plan and decides everything about the vineyard including which grapes to grow, how much to water, when to pick, how to process, etc. "

The Vine (Christ): The vine provides the life – the nutrients, the sap that produces the fruit. (Note that the sap is the Holy Spirit in this analogy).

The Vinedresser (The Father): The vinedresser is the one who has the plan and decides everything about the vineyard including which grapes to grow, how much to water, when to pick, how to process, etc. He thus is the one that I term "directing traffic" in all of our lives. He knows and wants to lead us. He is the vinedresser, and we are not.

The Branch: A tender and flexible branch. As a branch, we stay connected to the vine to produce fruit, but are not the vine or the vinedresser.

The Result: The desire of the vinedresser (the Father) is the fruit – more fruit, much fruit. He does not care about what the vineyard or the branches look like, but only the results: fruit.

> **bear**: to bring, bring to, bring forward
> **fruit**: effect
> **result**: greater in quantity, quality, superior, more excellent

The Choice: to remain, abide.

APART FROM CHRIST WE CAN DO NOTHING!

Repeat this over and over. Apart from abiding, we can do nothing. And it is our choice. We must decide that abiding is something we wish to learn and live out now and for the rest of our days.

Word Definition: **abide:** in reference to place—to sojourn, tarry, not to depart, to continue to be present, to be held, kept, continually

He clearly says that as each plays out their role, one of the key activities is for us (the branches) to be pruned. This means we are to cut back our activities that overwhelm us, so that we have margin, space in our lives for the process of fruit bearing to be full, luscious, enjoyable, and all that God wants it to be. Pruning is absolutely required for all healthy branches to be able to bear fruit. None of us is exempt, and we are to fully cooperate with this process. If not, we get tired and weary, and God will bring adversity to cause us to have a heart to cooperate so that we are pruned and able to enjoy our lives to the fullest.

As you consider pruning, what is the key to letting God create the good works since you are His workmanship? How does this practically work?

Read Ephesians 2:10:

[10] For we are his workmanship, created in Christ Jesus for good works, which God prepared beforehand, that we should walk in them.

_____

_____

_____

_____

_____

We are God's workmanship, and He's prepared beforehand the good works for His purpose to produce fruit. He already knows the things He wants you to go do and to be part of. He's already prepared ahead of time what He wants us to be doing. This always includes the truth of margin, which is really what's going to produce fruit. And there are specific things that we need to be involved in so that we give it our all and have the energy for it. It's not just the task, which is what we tend to think. It's you're thinking time. It's your prayer time. It's you're hearing time. It's you're believing time. All of that is involved with it, and you're investing time. And He wants you to enjoy it so that you have space, you have margin, and you will be able to handle the surprises, the new things that come up, which certainly will. There'll be people that will pop up who ask for your time. We must have margin to talk to anyone God needs us to.

He has His work ordained for you, and He wants you to enjoy the work, not to be tired or weary or burdened, but to have space and relaxation so you are living in peace and joy. We are to know and follow what He has ordained.

Word Definitions: **workmanship:** that which has been made, a work, of the works of God as Creator
good works: useful, pleasant, joyful, happy, excellent, distinguished, honorable—acts and activities planned by God
ordained: to prepare before, to make ready beforehand
walk: to make one's way, progress; to make use of opportunities

Seek Wisdom:

As we look at this verse again in light of pruning, what specifically are you to seek wisdom about in relation to your activities?

Read James 1:5–8:

5 If any of you lacks wisdom, let him ask God, who gives generously to all without reproach, and it will be given him. 6 But let him ask in faith, with no doubting, for the one who doubts is like a wave of the sea that is driven and tossed by the wind. 7 For that person must not suppose that he will receive anything from the Lord; 8 he is a double-minded man, unstable in all his ways.

_____

_____

_____

_____

_____

As we follow what He has ordained, this will require wisdom; we are to ask Him, and He'll give it to us liberally.

We need specific wisdom in a particular area. This is something that's very specific to each of us and has to do with our calendar and what activities we are to be involved in. This is the very definition of margin. We have to have space. Do we have space? Are we relaxed or tired, weary, and worn out?

List all your activities and begin building your time so it reflects what God would choose for you to be involved with. The absolutes include: time with your spouse, time with your kids, time for exercise, time for your business activity (which is quite a bit, but not to be too much, or all the time), time for errands and taking care of things like your home or special projects that need immediate attention, time for ministry and church/small group obligations, time for extended family, etc. Each of these will be specific to you.

We must recognize when something is taking more time than we thought. Or when someone is asking more of you than you committed. You may feel good and generous, but is it what God is asking you to do? If not, then other things will suffer, and that usually means your spouse, your time with God, or even a simple moment of relaxation. Have you stopped taking the Sabbath? Are you working more hours than you should? Are you tired and weary and have no margin—no peace, no joy, and are you no longer producing God's fruit?

Write this all down. Then have your spouse or friend or group evaluate and help sort out the truth. If someone says, "I only work till five o'clock," would the spouse agree? Or is he working till 5:00 only to return two hours later and ultimately spending no time with his family?

So, what's the truth? Start out with a clean list. The clean list is what God would have you do. What's absolutely God's priority at the moment? There are some absolutes in there: your personal time with God, that's absolute. You have to abide with God, which is critical. If you're married, you've got to spend time with your spouse. But what does that look like? Together, as a couple, you must decide what that looks like for the two of you. What do we enjoy doing? Are you dating? Taking time together? Are you walking together, taking time to process God's will together? That takes time. What about a child? You have a child who is involved in your life and typically young parents, you've got several to do's including driving them here and there. That's an activity that also must be accounted for on your list.

What is your work, and how much time do you need to spend at work? How much time should you be working? This also must be considered.

Take time to process with God and have others help you be accountable. In business, you may be accepting mediocrity or maybe you're doing too much. Or, maybe you are greedy, not wanting to hire a person because you want to make more money. But God is asking you to determine what is better: your time or more money.

Once you prioritize your list and your time, God promises to prune you to the best margin in life so that you will reach your sweet spot. You will begin to enjoy your life because you will be doing exactly what God wants you to do.

Then, two things will happen:

1. The things you're doing will grow. Every quarter, you will have to evaluate and say, what else do I need to change now? I need to do it differently because the things I did and are doing are growing and once again taking more of my time. Adjust this again by going to God for wisdom. Again, He will prune you, which is an ongoing process.

2. You will be asked to do new things, to add an activity, a new thing that you have not been doing but is something that is attractive to you, some new area of interest or opportunity to serve others, etc. It is something that seems like a good idea. At that moment, you need to go to God with this question: God, are you truly asking me to do that? If He is, then you will need to stop doing something else. But what is He asking you to stop? What is it? If you can't answer that question, then He's not asking you to do it. This will become clear as you process with your spouse.

Cooperate with God in pruning to reach margin, find your sweet spot, and stay there. It is absolutely His will and is the way for Him to bear fruit in your life. And it will be joyful and relaxing.

Rebuild your calendar with a new view toward priority, margin, rest, and Sabbath.

Tips for Rebuilding Your Calendar:

First, start from scratch and establish your key priorities: Time for God (Abiding), Word, Marriage, Kids, Grandkids, Friends, Ministry, Exercise, Recreation, and then assign how much fundamental time you are to give to each during the week.

Next, with what time is left, look at your list of activities, and work through what else you can bring into your task/calendar, and thus what else you need to slough.

Discuss how to slough off that which needs to be pruned. Then, take your calendar for the next two weeks and, with your spouse, establish your precise calendar schedule. Also, discuss new commitments like dating, time for sharing your abiding, travel, vacations, etc.

Now let's turn our attention to adversity that is caused by us—by our selfishness, especially when it goes to discipline and judgment.

SELFISHNESS/DISCIPLINE/JUDGEMENT:

To overcome adversity that we have caused ourselves—selfishness, discipline, and judgment, we must return to the Kingdom of God through our only remedy available to us: Repentance.

Let's consider selfishness, discipline, and judgment. They all go together because the remedy is the same.

Fundamentally, what is the remedy? Repentance. You must go back to the Kingdom and say what? You must recognize that you've been trying to do everything on your own but now remember that you need to turn back to God. This is repentance: to turn around and come back. And that's the only answer. It doesn't matter whether you're in your first part of the adversity because you caused it; or in deeper adversity, because you're in discipline; or the deepest adversity, because you're in judgment. The remedy anywhere along that path is the same: Apologize and repent. The good news is that when you do that, God says what? He is thrilled and ready to fix things again. Great. Let's go. Let Him fix it.

What caused selfishness, and how was it overcome? What does this mean to us regarding how to repent and get into the right relationship to have God resolve our adversity?

Read Romans 5:12–21:

Death in Adam, Life in Christ

12 Therefore, just as sin came into the world through one man, and death through sin, and so death spread to all men[a] because all sinned— 13 for sin indeed was in the world before the law was given, but sin is not counted where there is no law.14 Yet death reigned from Adam to Moses, even over those whose sinning was not like the transgression of Adam, who was a type of the one who was to come.

> [15] But the free gift is not like the trespass. For if many died through one man's trespass, much more have the grace of God and the free gift by the grace of that one man Jesus Christ abounded for many. [16] And the free gift is not like the result of that one man's sin. For the judgment following one trespass brought condemnation, but the free gift following many trespasses brought justification. [17] For if, because of one man's trespass, death reigned through that one man, much more will those who receive the abundance of grace and the free gift of righteousness reign in life through the one man Jesus Christ.
>
> [18] Therefore, as one trespass[b] led to condemnation for all men, so one act of righteousness[c] leads to justification and life for all men. [19] For as by the one man's disobedience the many were made sinners, so by the one man's obedience the many will be made righteous. [20] Now the law came in to increase the trespass, but where sin increased, grace abounded all the more, [21] so that, as sin reigned in death, grace also might reign through righteousness leading to eternal life through Jesus Christ our Lord.

_____

_____

_____

_____

_____

The scriptures lay out the basis of repentance—the issue of self-will, the flesh. The problem of adversity happened because of one man's and one woman's sin which was what? Rebellion. I will do what I like. I choose what I want. I disobey what God instructed. Adam and Eve set the whole thing into a mess and we're participating in that mess. All this happened because of them, and the nature that we carry is theirs—the flesh and the ongoing struggle with self-centeredness. But there is good news. The power to overcome all that came through this sin is Jesus and overcoming self-will.

Adam gave up his rights. He chose his self-will and brought about destruction that allowed the world to be controlled by Satan and entropy. Jesus conquered this, overcame through obedience to go to the cross, which He demonstrated with His willingness first to come to Earth, and to overcome what happened in the Garden of Eden.

In John, Chapter 10, Christ tells us that He's going to go to His own death, and that the Father was not going to help Him at all. This is unlike all the other times when Jesus got His power from the Father. He did what His Father told Him. This time, it's going to be His battle of the will. So, He goes to the battle in the garden. He goes in and He prays, and He knows He must battle through this and even says: Father, you're so sovereign because I know your sovereign creativity and ability to make anything happen. Come up with Plan B. Could you come up Plan B? The Father declines. Christ walks out of the garden and says, not My will be done, but Yours. Why did He go back in? He didn't have it settled. It was intellectual. He knew in His heart it wasn't settled, that He was not completely sold out to finishing this work. And so, He had to go back in to process a little longer. He asked that the cup pass from Him, as He didn't want to do what was coming. When He came out, He agreed that God's will would be done, and not His. Why did He go in a third time? It still wasn't finished. It still wasn't settled in the soul to victory. He gets to such an intensity of the battle that His forehead blood vessels burst, and He sweats drops of blood—it's that intense. Finally, He emerges and says it's settled: Your will be done, not mine. And then He marches to His death. Did He ever struggle anymore? No. Now, He had settled it because He had the victory of overcoming, of winning the battle of the self-will.

And this is what Paul is showing us: by one man, it's all been lost, and by one man, it's gained back—through the battle of the self. So now that He's won that battle, we then join Him in the Kingdom of God to have Him overcome our adversity, where He promises He has and will overcome it for us. How do we join Him? What must we do? Surrender. We must surrender our will now. But can we just go through the garden, the death of self once? No. How often do we have to do this? All the time.

And because it's the battle of the flesh, if you don't follow Him in the Spirit and surrender your will, you default back to the flesh and do not join Him in the Kingdom where He will resolve this adversity. This is why you have to surrender and to repent. And the only place the victory can occur is with Him in the Kingdom of God. That's where all the authority occurs. Satan has the authority of the world. Is it superior to God's? No. Where is God's superior authority? In His Kingdom, which you have access to. By what? Surrendering to His will. We can live in both places. And that's why He says you have to repent and surrender. The victory has been won. In His Kingdom, there is no power of Satan. Through surrender, and only through surrender, do we join Him there.
Christ's surrender resolved the issue of self.

Word Definitions:

sin: that which is done wrong, an offense, a violation of the divine law in thought or in act

enter: entrance into any condition, state of things, society

death: in the widest sense, death comprising all the miseries arising from sin, as well physical death as the loss of a life consecrated to God and blessed in Him on Earth, to be followed by wretchedness in hell

grace: that which affords joy, pleasure, delight, sweetness, charm, loveliness: grace of speech, good will, loving-kindness, favor, of the merciful kindness by which God, exerting his holy influence upon souls, turns them to Christ, keeps, strengthens, increases them in Christian faith, knowledge, affection, and kindles them to the exercise of the Christian virtue

act of righteousness/obedience: compliance, submission, rendered to anyone's counsels

What is the process of repentance? What does it result in, and why is this so important to our process of Him resolving our adversity?

> **Read 1 John 1:9:**
>
> 9 If we confess our sins, he is faithful and just to forgive us our sins and to cleanse us from all unrighteousness.

_____

_____

_____

_____

_____

When you've caused your own adversity, the remedy is simply to come back through repentance. If you confess your sin (self-will), He is faithful and will forgive us our sins and cleanse us from all un-righteousness. How fast does that occur? Instantly. He says, "Welcome back, let's go and let me now resolve all your adversity." A simple response of repentance is "I'm sorry. I come back, I return, I come back to you into that relationship where the power is." He welcomes us back and will then resolve our adversity.

LESSON 6:
OVERCOMING ADVERSITIES (CONTINUED)

Word Definitions: **confess:** to say the same thing as another, (i.e., to agree with, assent)
faithful: of persons who show themselves faithful in the transaction
cleanse: to free from guilt of sin, to purify, to consecrate by cleansing or purifying

Identify the progression to a life of fruit and resolution to adversity. What is the key to having it fulfilled for us? (It is a paradox.)

Read Romans 6:7, 18, 22:

[7] For one who has died has been set free[a] from sin.

[18] and, having been set free from sin, have become slaves of righteousness.

[22] But now that you have been set free from sin and have become slaves of God, the fruit you get leads to sanctification and its end, eternal life.

_____

_____

_____

_____

_____

Through this process of surrender, we experience a wonderful progression that leads to freedom and resolution.

1. We have already been set free from sin, which is past tense, already done. So, there's still an issue of: Why do I struggle with sin, with self-will? This leads to:

2. Having been set free from sin (which gives us the constant ability to have relationship with God in His Kingdom where the power is), we are to become slaves of righteousness. That's the answer. We always have a choice to make. Do you become a slave to self and still experience the burden of sin and the consequences of adversity? Or do you become a slave to righteousness and surrender your life to Him where He overcomes adversity. In order to have the freedom and the joy of victory, you have to become a slave. It's an interesting conundrum. If I want the freedom and the victory, I have to become a slave. While you become a slave to Christ, you gain the freedom and the victory.

3. Now that you have been set free from sin and have become slaves of God, you receive sanctification and the fruit of holiness, which is victory with Him. The fruit of the holiness is the victory, the overcoming. As you become a slave, you get the fruit of victory, the resolution of the adversity. You do not achieve it on your own, but receive it as a result, the fruit.

Word Definitions:

freed: to declare, pronounce, one to be just, righteous, or such as he ought to be
become slaves: metaph. give myself wholly to one's needs and service, make myself a bondman to him
fruit: that which originates or comes from something, an effect, result
holiness: sanctification of heart and life

Upon our repentance, He immediately restores us back to fellowship, and the vibrant life of the Spirit. However, depending upon the length of time we have been away from His Kingdom life and His Covenant blessings, we may have experienced a certain level of severe adverse consequences that need restoration. At this point, we first must believe that He will restore us from these adversities, so that we can remain in peace, hope, encouragement, and in the abiding relationship as we learn to take authority against these adversities while the restoration takes place (which depending upon the severity may take some time).

What are God's promises to restoring us from our adversities that we caused? Why is this so important for our process, and what can we expect?

Read Ezekiel 36:33–38:

[33] "Thus says the Lord God: On the day that I cleanse you from all your iniquities, I will cause the cities to be inhabited, and the waste places shall be rebuilt.[34] And the land that was desolate shall be tilled, instead of being the desolation that it was in the sight of all who passed by. [35] And they will say, 'This land that was desolate has become like the garden of Eden, and the waste and desolate and ruined cities are now fortified and inhabited.'[36] Then the nations that are left all around you shall know that I am the Lord; I have rebuilt the ruined places and replanted that which was desolate. I am the Lord; I have spoken, and I will do it.

[37] "Thus says the Lord God: This also I will let the house of Israel ask me to do for them: to increase their people like a flock. [38] Like the flock for sacrifices,[a] like the flock at Jerusalem during her appointed feasts, so shall the waste cities be filled with flocks of people. Then they will know that I am the Lord."

_____

_____

_____

_____

_____

Now that you've repented, He promises restoration. Thus says the Lord God: On the day that I cleanse you from all your iniquities, I will also enable you to dwell in the cities again, and the ruins of those places shall be rebuilt. The desolate land shall be tilled instead of lying desolate. The land that was desolate has become like the Garden of Eden and the wasted, desolate, and ruined cities are now fortified and inhabited. Then the nations, which are left all around you, shall know that the Lord has rebuilt the ruined places and planted what was desolate. He has spoken it, and because He has spoken it, He will do it.

He says: What has been wasted, ruined will be restored to be like the Garden of Eden. I restore it, rebuild it, and actually make it even better than it was. This means that you caused the ruin. But now that you've repented, what will God do? He'll fix it and restore it back to the fullness of all the beautiful things that He has promised, as He so ordains.

He does not want us to live in guilt because we caused it or stay in the failure with the thought that you deserve to live in the failure. He just says: Now that you're back, regardless of whether you're in the consequence of your own decisions, or discipline, or even judgment—now that you're back and you have a heart to walk with Me, let's go. Let's restart, and I will restore everything to beauty. Another wonder of the Gospel is that God can do it now.

Word Definitions: **cleansed:** to purify, be clean morally, made clean

rebuilt: restored

waste: place laid waste, ruin, desolation

rebuilt: to be rebuilt, established (of restored exiles) (figuratively), established (made permanent)

desolated: be deflowered, be deserted, be appalled

garden: enclosed garden (figuratively of a bride)

When we are stuck and seemingly have no options for resolution, what does God promise? Why is this so important to our heart and to the process of resolution?

Read Psalm 40:1–8:

My Help and My Deliverer
To the choirmaster. A Psalm of David.

40 I waited patiently for the Lord;
   he inclined to me and heard my cry.
2 He drew me up from the pit of destruction,
   out of the miry bog,
and set my feet upon a rock,
   making my steps secure.
3 He put a new song in my mouth,
   a song of praise to our God.
Many will see and fear,
   and put their trust in the Lord.
4 Blessed is the man who makes
   the Lord his trust,
who does not turn to the proud,
   to those who go astray after a lie!
5 You have multiplied, O Lord my God,
   your wondrous deeds and your thoughts toward us;
   none can compare with you!
I will proclaim and tell of them,
   yet they are more than can be told.
6 In sacrifice and offering you have not delighted,
   but you have given me an open ear.[a]
Burnt offering and sin offering
   you have not required.
7 Then I said, "Behold, I have come;
   in the scroll of the book it is written of me:
8 I delight to do your will, O my God;
   your law is within my heart."

_____

_____

_____

_____

_____

He is giving you a picture that you're stuck in the mud, and as far as you're concerned, there doesn't seem to be any way out of it. You're caught in a pickle. You're caught in an enigma, a double bind, and you can't escape. The circumstances are just too difficult. And God says, "If you walk with me, I will take care of that. I'll give you this incredible solution, and I'll get you back up on a rock and assist you."

Likely this will take His supernatural work. "I will take you out of the clay and take you out of the conundrum, out of the mess and put you on solid ground; I desire to, and I can. I'm going to do something unusual that only I can do because I can do things that are beyond you and the natural. That's My power. I can overcome it with supernatural work. And your ultimate response as you experience this resolution is that you delight in My will. It will become a part of your life as you receive the wonderful truth of this.

This is God's heart for all of us.

Word Definitions: **brought up:** be taken up, be brought up, be taken away
set: to be firm, be stable, be established, to be set up, be fixed
rock: a stronghold of Jehovah, of security
delight in: take pleasure in, desire, be pleased with

As we are seeking resolution to our adversities, what else does God promise, and why is this so important to our process of realizing resolution?

Read Jeremiah 32:36–41; 33:3–14:

They Shall Be My People; I Will Be Their God
36 "Now therefore thus says the Lord, the God of Israel, concerning this city of which you say, 'It is given into the hand of the king of Babylon by sword, by famine, and by pestilence': 37 Behold, I will gather them from all the countries to which I drove them in my anger and my wrath and in great indignation. I will bring them back to this place, and I will make them dwell in safety. 38 And they shall be my people, and I will be their God. 39 I will give them one heart and one way, that they may fear me forever, for their own good and the good of their children after them. 40 I will make with them an everlasting covenant, that I will not turn away from doing good to them. And I will put the fear of me in their hearts, that they may not turn from me. 41 I will rejoice in doing them good, and I will plant them in this land in faithfulness, with all my heart and all my soul.

LESSON 6:
OVERCOMING ADVERSITIES (CONTINUED)

3 Call to me and I will answer you, and will tell you great and hidden things that you have not known. 4 For thus says the Lord, the God of Israel, concerning the houses of this city and the houses of the kings of Judah that were torn down to make a defense against the siege mounds and against the sword: 5 They are coming in to fight against the Chaldeans and to fill them[a] with the dead bodies of men whom I shall strike down in my anger and my wrath, for I have hidden my face from this city because of all their evil. 6 Behold, I will bring to it health and healing, and I will heal them and reveal to them abundance of prosperity and security. 7 I will restore the fortunes of Judah and the fortunes of Israel, and rebuild them as they were at first. 8 I will cleanse them from all the guilt of their sin against me, and I will forgive all the guilt of their sin and rebellion against me. 9 And this city[b] shall be to me a name of joy, a praise and a glory before all the nations of the earth who shall hear of all the good that I do for them. They shall fear and tremble because of all the good and all the prosperity I provide for it.

10 "Thus says the Lord: In this place of which you say, 'It is a waste without man or beast,' in the cities of Judah and the streets of Jerusalem that are desolate, without man or inhabitant or beast, there shall be heard again 11 the voice of mirth and the voice of gladness, the voice of the bridegroom and the voice of the bride, the voices of those who sing, as they bring thank offerings to the house of the Lord:
"'Give thanks to the Lord of hosts,
    for the Lord is good,
    for his steadfast love endures forever!'
For I will restore the fortunes of the land as at first, says the Lord.
12 "Thus says the Lord of hosts: In this place that is waste, without man or beast, and in all of its cities, there shall again be habitations of shepherds resting their flocks. 13 In the cities of the hill country, in the cities of the Shephelah, and in the cities of the Negeb, in the land of Benjamin, the places about Jerusalem, and in the cities of Judah, flocks shall again pass under the hands of the one who counts them, says the Lord.

The Lord's Eternal Covenant with David
14 "Behold, the days are coming, declares the Lord, when I will fulfill the promise I made to the house of Israel and the house of Judah.

_____

_____

_____

_____

_____

God says: I'll do it, and I'll restore them—with all My heart, with all My soul. I'm going to make all this happen. Now that they're repenting, I'm going to bring it all back to them and restart all.

Part of the key to this is for us to demonstrate our surrender by calling out to Him for answers and expecting to hear things that we could not possibly know on our own or with our own wisdom. He says: I'll give you a great many things that you do not know. And then He promises what this will bring to us:

1. Health and healing.

2. Our restoration. Our rebuilding.

3. Great, wonderful, marvelous things.

He says He will absolutely perform everything that He says He will—it will happen. We can count on it. So, if you need a decision, or need guidance, or need direction about this adversity—even though you know you caused it yourself— you are to call out, expect answers that you cannot receive on your own, and know that He will restore, for He has promised to perform what He speaks.

Word Definitions:

safety: security

good (everlasting Covenant): pleasant, agreeable (adjective), agreeable (to the senses), pleasant (to the higher nature), excellent (of its kind), rich, valuable in estimation, appropriate, becoming better (comparative), glad, happy, prosperous great and mighty things: secrets, mysteries, inaccessible things (substantive)

healing: restoration

abundance: excess, copiousness

reveal: uncover

truth: firmness, faithfulness, truth (noun feminine), sureness, reliability

peace: shalom

cleanse: purify, restore

honor: beauty, splendor, glory

prosperity: completeness, soundness, welfare, peace

gladness: joy, mirth, gaiety

Let's look next at the attacks of the enemy. What is our response when we know we are being attacked (not general adversity, not a test of faith, and not something caused by our own selfishness)?

ATTACKS OF THE ENEMY

When we are attacked by the enemy, what are our two responses, and what is the result? What should we expect about this adversity?

Read James 4:7:

[7] Submit yourselves therefore to God. Resist the devil, and he will flee from you.

_____

_____

_____

_____

_____

When being attacked, our first call is to submit to God, the Father, asking: What are You going to do? What are You going to say about this, and what are You going to lead me to? And then resist (stand against) this attack, which we will learn to identify.

And the enemy will flee, he will exit. This attack is going to go away. That's simple. Why? Because when you've submitted to God, you're in the Kingdom. Victory is already of the Kingdom. The enemy has no access to you so he can't complete his attack. He has no power. You have all the authority over him. Complete authority and victory. It has already been won. He's already disarmed. Victory is sure. This is not a battle of equals. If this is an attack of the enemy, you have complete authority to chase them basically out of this attack. And it has to end completely and quickly.

But remember that it is important to understand the difference between an attack from the enemy or something you caused yourself. The remedies are different, so it is important to know the source. If it is an attack, we are to submit and resist as this remedy is absolute and powerful.

LESSON 6:
OVERCOMING ADVERSITIES (CONTINUED)

Word Definitions: **subject:** to arrange under, to subordinate, put in subjection, to subject one's self, obey, to submit to one's control, to yield to one's admonition or advice, to obey, be subject

resist: to set one's self against, to withstand, oppose, to set against

flee: to flee away, vanish

As we are to put on the armor of God and not fight the enemy with our own power, what are these elements, and what do they mean? What will happen if we use these weapons?

Read Ephesians 6:10–20:

The Whole Armor of God

[10] Finally, be strong in the Lord and in the strength of his might. [11] Put on the whole armor of God, that you may be able to stand against the schemes of the devil. [12] For we do not wrestle against flesh and blood, but against the rulers, against the authorities, against the cosmic powers over this present darkness, against the spiritual forces of evil in the heavenly places. [13] Therefore take up the whole armor of God, that you may be able to withstand in the evil day, and having done all, to stand firm. [14] Stand therefore, having fastened on the belt of truth, and having put on the breastplate of righteousness, [15] and, as shoes for your feet, having put on the readiness given by the gospel of peace. [16] In all circumstances take up the shield of faith, with which you can extinguish all the flaming darts of the evil one; [17] and take the helmet of salvation, and the sword of the Spirit, which is the word of God, [18] praying at all times in the Spirit, with all prayer and supplication. To that end, keep alert with all perseverance, making supplication for all the saints, [19] and also for me, that words may be given to me in opening my mouth boldly to proclaim the mystery of the gospel, [20] for which I am an ambassador in chains, that I may declare it boldly, as I ought to speak.

_____

_____

_____

_____

_____

Paul tells us to put on the armor, which is God, because that's the power. If you try to do this in the natural, what's going to happen to you? You're going to get beat up because then you're going out into the enemy's kingdom of the flesh and he's got you.

1. Put on the Belt of Truth. What this means is that you need to know everything about this, the whole truth, what's going on, what's the situation, what's happening. What is it that I need to know about me, about them, about the situation, the facts, every piece of truth I can get? Am I open to receiving the truth? What's the truth? What's the truth? What's the truth? Am I open to anything You want to show me that I need to understand spiritual truth—even if that means that You reveal my heart of anger or my heart of resentment? Is there something that I really shouldn't be doing?

2. Put on the Breastplate of Righteousness. Who is righteous? Jesus Christ. If you're going to go into this battle, then you better step into Christ. Are you in Christ? It's not your righteousness, it's His righteousness. And this is your protector. Are you in Christ, and are you having that deep, abiding relationship with Him? What are You going to do? What are You going to say? How are You going to lead me? How are You going to guide me?

3. Put the Gospel of Peace on your feet. What do you do with your feet? You go into battle. Before you go to battle, make sure that you are in peace. You're not riled up, you're not angry, you're not frustrated, you're not irritated. Because if you are, it isn't going to go well for you. If you're not in peace, go back to step one. What's the truth? Go back to stepping back into Christ, in other words, don't go any farther, but go back through the process and return to peace.

4. Take up the Shield of Faith. And this is just a small shield. You are being attacked with arrows of falsities or things that God has already revealed to you, so these will have no effect. Block these with faith, by believing the truth. This is a defensive act, because you're extinguishing darts that are coming at you, and your faith is blocking them. You will be protected.

5. Put on the Helmet of Salvation. What is salvation? It's deliverance, health, healing, wholeness. It's a helmet that covers your whole head—including your mind. You will have clarity of thought, the power to know that God will act, and that all will be resolved. You will be whole and delivered from this attack. You have the authority and the power and will exercise it. There will be no fear, but faith and confidence. You will submit to God and resist this attack; and the enemy will flee. The attack will be over.

6. Put on the Sword of the Word. Until now, you have asked for protection…protect me, protect me, protect me. You feel ready to go. And then you take the Sword of the Word, which is: How dare he defy the army of the living God. He has been defeated. You take the authority, and this no longer will stand. And you're going to overcome this in the authority of Christ. You will speak against this. The enemy has no right here. Absolutely not. And you pray against it, and you stand.

So, you pray, and you persevere. You stand against it and don't let it continue. This is not of God, and we have the power against it, and you'll see it leave absolutely.

Word Definitions:

armor: complete armor, includes shield, sword, lance, helmet, greaves, and breastplate

withstand: resist, oppose, to set against

perseverance: steadfastly attentive unto, to give unremitting care to a thing

utterance: logos (what God speaks)

stand: make firm, fix establish, to cause a person or a thing to keep his or its place

- **Belt of Truth (truth):** firmness, faithfulness, truth (noun feminine), sureness, reliability, all truth

- **Breastplate of Righteousness (righteousness):** integrity, virtue, purity of life, rightness, correctness of thinking, feeling, and acting

- **Gospel of Peace on our feet:** harmony, concord, security, safety, prosperity, felicity, (because peace and harmony make and keep things safe and prosperous)

- **Shield of Faith:**
  shield: full body protection, not arm shield
  faith: conviction of the truth of anything, belief; in the NT of a conviction or belief respecting man's relationship to God and divine things, generally with the included idea of trust and holy fervor born of faith and joined with it
  quench: extinguish
  fiery: indignant
  darts: missiles that are thrown without caring where they fall

- **The Helmet of Salvation (salvation):** complete, wholeness, deliverance

- **The Sword of the Word:**
  sword: straight, offensive weapon for thrusting
  Word: Rhema
  prayer: addressed to God
  watching: be sleepless, keep awake, watch, to be circumspect, attentive, ready

LESSON 6:
OVERCOMING ADVERSITIES (CONTINUED)

Based upon the adversaries you noted that you are encountering right now and that you described in detail on the first day, and the effect they are having on you at this moment, review each step and categorize where they fit regarding the source of the adversity. Remember, the adversity will fall into one of these areas:

- General Adversity
- Trial of God
- Pruning
- Selfishness, Discipline, Judgment
- Attacks of the Enemy – Stand and come against

> " The power to overcome truly resides through our life in the spiritual dimension of the Kingdom as we operate in the kingdom of the world where we are experiencing the adversity."

So, we have discerned what kind of adversity this is, and we have taken the appropriate initial action and approach:

1. General Adversity – Staying in peace, following the Father's wisdom

2. Trial of God – Going to fully cooperate

3. Pruning – Going to fully cooperate and work at margin, release of burdens

4. Selfishness, Discipline, Judgment – Repented; returned to Kingdom

5. Attacks of the Enemy – Stand and come against

In each situation now, we will have types of adversity, different levels and severity of adversity, and different levels of spiritual forces against us. At this point, we are already fully living in the Kingdom of God or have returned to living in the Kingdom of God where our authority rests. The power to overcome truly resides through our life in the spiritual dimension of the Kingdom as we operate in the kingdom of the world where we are experiencing the adversity.

TYPES OF ADVERSITY:

1. RELATIONSHIP ISSUES:

- First, go to, stay in forgiveness.

Why is it so important to go to forgiveness? How does this free us up?

Read Mark 11:20–25:

The Lesson from the Withered Fig Tree
[20] As they passed by in the morning, they saw the fig tree withered away to its roots. [21] And Peter remembered and

said to him, "Rabbi, look! The fig tree that you cursed has withered." [22] And Jesus answered them, "Have faith in God.[23] Truly, I say to you, whoever says to this mountain, 'Be taken up and thrown into the sea,' and does not doubt in his heart, but believes that what he says will come to pass, it will be done for him. [24] Therefore I tell you, whatever you ask in prayer, believe that you have received[a] it, and it will be yours. [25] And whenever you stand praying, forgive, if you have anything against anyone, so that your Father also who is in heaven may forgive you your trespasses."[b]

_____

_____

_____

_____

_____

As we are learning powerful prayer through belief and declaration, He reminds us that if you have unforgiveness in your heart toward somebody, to stop praying because you've separated yourself from Him. And His nature no longer is operating in you—you are in the flesh, outside of His Kingdom. Thus, you are to immediately get back to forgiveness. It's okay that you have anger toward this person who has hurt or harmed you, but you need to go to forgiveness, which is about your heart between God and you, about your relationship with God, and the freedom He wants you to enjoy and live out.

Word Definition: **forgive:** to let go, let alone, let be

On what basis do we go to forgiveness? Why again is this so important?

Read Ephesians 4:25–32:

[25] Therefore, having put away falsehood, let each one of you speak the truth with his neighbor, for we are members one of another. [26] Be angry and do not sin; do not let the sun go down on your anger, [27] and give no opportunity to the devil.[28] Let the thief no longer steal, but rather let him labor, doing honest work with his own hands, so that he may have something to share with anyone in need.[29] Let no corrupting talk come out of your mouths, but only such as is

LESSON 7:
TAKING AUTHORITY AGAINST THE ADVERSITY

> good for building up, as fits the occasion, that it may give grace to those who hear. [30] And do not grieve the Holy Spirit of God, by whom you were sealed for the day of redemption. [31] Let all bitterness and wrath and anger and clamor and slander be put away from you, along with all malice. [32] Be kind to one another, tenderhearted, forgiving one another, as God in Christ forgave you.

_____

_____

_____

_____

_____

Be angry and do not sin. Is anger a sin? No, it's natural. This person's opposing you, is against you, is harming you. This is one of the tricks the enemy uses to thwart God's will. Trying to prevent you from moving forward or having success, having freedom because you take anger to sin. But in your anger, don't let it go to malice. Don't let it go to revenge. He says the key, which is found in verse 32, is to forgive on the same basis that Christ has forgiven you. On what basis did God forgive you? His own nature—the nature of love and forgiveness. Did you deserve it? No. Did you do anything to earn it? No. Remember, He's talking only about forgiveness and not reconciliation. He's saying forgive them so that your heart is free. And that's the first element of this process. Once you've forgiven them and have worked through that process with God, then you must deal with the issue of opposition. That person may still be hurting you or causing you pain. Or, they're still trying to prevent your success. But you have forgiven them. Now what? How do you handle that? We will consider this in the next section.

Word Definition: **forgive:** to grant forgiveness, to pardon

- Understand truth of Covenant and God's justice, sure wrath.

What do I understand about the Covenant regarding relationships, especially those who oppose me? Why is this important?

Read Genesis 12:1–3:

The Call of Abram

12 Now the Lord said[a] to Abram, "Go from your country[b] and your kindred and your father's house to the land that I will show you. [2] And I will make of you a great nation, and I will bless you and make your name great, so that you will be a blessing. [3] I will bless those who bless you, and him who dishonors you I will curse, and in you all the families of the earth shall be blessed."[c]

_____

_____

_____

_____

_____

The essence of our relationship with God, which is eternal and always operating, is the Covenant: "I'm going to bless you to make you a blessing. I'm going to bless those who bless you. But I'm also going to curse those who curse you." But let's be clear. What He means by those who curse you aren't those who just disagree with you. Instead, it's those who are not willing to process with you on a path toward reconciliation and resolution.

These are the people who say: I continue to oppose you because I want my will, and I don't care what you want. I don't care that we could seek God's will together or what would be healthy for both of us. And then God says: They're cursed. Of course, the key is that we never want to be on the other side of that. Are you always willing to go to forgiveness, and then sit down and process it? If we are willing to process with God, we will never be cursed. Others may not be willing, and they are cursed. So, what do we do with that? Let's go to this next.

Word Definition: **curse:** lay under a curse, put a curse on

For people who continue to oppose us, continue to harm us, how do we handle them, so we are not trapped by their unhealthiness? What does this look like practically, and how does it really work?

Read Romans 12:9–20 and Proverbs 20:22:

Marks of the True Christian

9 Let love be genuine. Abhor what is evil; hold fast to what is good. 10 Love one another with brotherly affection. Outdo one another in showing honor. 11 Do not be slothful in zeal, be fervent in spirit,[a] serve the Lord. 12 Rejoice in hope, be patient in tribulation, be constant in prayer. 13 Contribute to the needs of the saints and seek to show hospitality.

14 Bless those who persecute you; bless and do not curse them. 15 Rejoice with those who rejoice, weep with those who weep. 16 Live in harmony with one another. Do not be haughty, but associate with the lowly.[b] Never be wise in your own sight. 17 Repay no one evil for evil, but give thought to do what is honorable in the sight of all. 18 If possible, so far as it depends on you, live peaceably with all. 19 Beloved, never avenge yourselves, but leave it[c] to the wrath of God, for it is written, "Vengeance is mine, I will repay, says the Lord." 20 To the contrary, "if your enemy is hungry, feed him; if he is thirsty, give him something to drink; for by so doing you will heap burning coals on his head."

22 Do not say, "I will repay evil";
   wait for the Lord, and he will deliver you.

_____

_____

_____

_____

_____

When people continue to oppose us and are not willing to process with us, we are reminded in these verses how we are to walk with God so that we do not cause further adversity. It also shows how we further experience God's promised resolution to the adversity. We are to be respectful at all times. We can be respectful because we have gone to forgiveness and do not carry any bitterness or edginess toward this other person. Further, we in no way try to fix this ourselves and take revenge; or come against this other party that's coming against us. We don't curse them. We don't take vengeance. We don't come up with a scheme to manipulate to get our way. We simply act in a respectful way as far as is concerning us. The verses say to make every effort to resolve it, to live peaceably, which is to offer an opportunity to sit down and work it through. It doesn't say give in. It says, work it through with integrity as you're working toward truth. These verses are about how to do it, how to approach it with a heart of forgiveness. What's the truth? Let's see if we can work this out. Hey, what you're doing is really harming me. What you're doing is coming against me. This can be a business situation, a ministry situation, a personal situation. It doesn't matter, we must try to work it through with integrity.

You have made an attempt, and they either blame you (unwilling to process truth) or refuse completely to even process with you. In other words, they say: I have no care what you think or feel. I'm coming against you. I do not care about any consequences to you. I want what I want, and I am going to keep acting this way to get it.

God then says, "Get out of the way and leave room for My wrath." Based on the Covenant, God says they're cursed. Justice will be served because he says vengeance will be done. The truth is the truth, and justice will be served. It might not be as fast as you want it to happen, but don't worry. Justice will be served. Vengeance is God's. You get out of the way. Move on. God will take care of this.

And then He makes this interesting statement: Instead of cursing them, which He says is His role, not yours, bless them. That's an interesting thing. God said He's going to curse them, which is automatic. How can we bless them if God is cursing them? This is really profound. The only way that anybody who is cursed can be blessed and have the curse reversed is by the cross. And based upon Christ's work on the cross what must we do to have that curse reversed? Repent and go to the truth—accept Christ as our Lord and Savior –and then we are blessed and step into the Covenant that He will bless us to make us a blessing—if we stay walking with Him in His Kingdom and surrender our will to His. So, we are to pray that this other party repents and can stop the curse—the only remedy available to have the curse reversed. We are thus to have God's heart, which is not to have someone continually cursed (which they are since justice will be served) but to repent and stop the curse and then step into blessing. We are to join God in that same nature of forgiveness and love—not accepting their ongoing harm to us, since they are cursed, but living in the freedom of not carrying the burden of this, and moving on with our lives, which will be blessed.

The only thing we can do to go from a curse to a blessing is to repent.

That's the only thing that reverses the curse.

The only way to get them to repent, if they choose not to, is to pray for them so that they, too, might be blessed.

Word Definitions: **abhor:** dislike, have a horror of

cleave: to join or fasten firmly together, to join one's self to

good: pleasant, agreeable (to the senses); pleasant (to the higher nature), excellent, rich, valuable in estimation: glad, happy, prosperous

affection: prone to love, loving tenderly

bless: to consecrate a thing with solemn prayers

persecute: to harass, trouble, molest one; to be mistreated, suffer persecution on account of something; curse, doom, imprecate evil upon

recompense: to deliver, to give away for one's own profit what is one's own, to sell; to pay off, discharge what is due, repay

honest: beautiful, handsome, excellent, eminent, choice, surpassing, precious, useful, suitable, commendable, admirable

avenge: to punish a person for a thing

vengeance: a revenging, punishment; meeting out of justice; doing justice to all parties. The word also has the sense of acquittal and carries the sense of vindication

repay: in a bad sense, penalty and vengeance

- Know the only remedy for enemy's blessing is repentance.

- In absence of repentance, stand on God's promise to protect and not allow the enemy to defeat/overcome you.

How do we pray regarding those who continually are working to harm us, come against us? What does God promise about this? Can we expect this? Why is this important?

Read Psalm 54:1–7:

The Lord Upholds My Life
To the choirmaster: with stringed instruments. A Maskil[a] of David, when the Ziphites went and told Saul, "Is not David hiding among us?"
54 O God, save me by your name,
　　and vindicate me by your might.

LESSON 7:
TAKING AUTHORITY AGAINST THE ADVERSITY

> [2] O God, hear my prayer;
>   give ear to the words of my mouth.
> [3] For strangers[b] have risen against me;
>   ruthless men seek my life;
>   they do not set God before themselves. Selah
> [4] Behold, God is my helper;
>   the Lord is the upholder of my life.
> [5] He will return the evil to my enemies;
>   in your faithfulness put an end to them.
> [6] With a freewill offering I will sacrifice to you;
>   I will give thanks to your name, O Lord, for it is good.
> [7] For he has delivered me from every trouble,
>   and my eye has looked in triumph on my enemies.

_____

_____

_____

_____

_____

For those who are against you and continue to attempt to harm you, you don't just leave it and say, well, whatever happens, happens. You now are in forgiveness, and without you taking action in revenge or attempting to fix this yourself, go to prayer. Pray to the Father to deliver you from the trouble. Do not figure out a way to win this battle and jump right back in the flesh, back into the fray. If you do so, you will throw everything you did out the window and bring about more adversity. You have walked away from God's protection and are under the authority and power of the enemy where consequences are going to get worse. Instead, let it go and say to the Father: "You're going to have to take care of it, and I will listen and follow." He may give you a piece of instruction or a piece of wisdom or suggest a step He'd like you to take. But He will deliver you, and your enemy will not succeed. We can count on it. Absolutely.

Word Definitions: **oppressors**: awe-inspiring, terror-striking, awesome, terrifying, ruthless, mighty
to put an end to: terminate, to be ended, be annihilated, be exterminated
deliver: rescue, save

Further, what can we expect God to do for us regarding the adversity that is being caused by people against us? Why is this important for us and our resolution of adversity?

Read Psalm 40:11–17:

11 As for you, O Lord, you will not restrain
    your mercy from me;
your steadfast love and your faithfulness will
    ever preserve me!
12 For evils have encompassed me
    beyond number;
my iniquities have overtaken me,
    and I cannot see;
they are more than the hairs of my head;
    my heart fails me.
13 Be pleased, O Lord, to deliver me!
    O Lord, make haste to help me!
14 Let those be put to shame and disappointed altogether
    who seek to snatch away my life,
let those be turned back and brought to dishonor
    who delight in my hurt!
15 Let those be appalled because of their shame
    who say to me, "Aha, Aha!"
16 But may all who seek you
    rejoice and be glad in you;
may those who love your salvation
    say continually, "Great is the Lord!"
17 As for me, I am poor and needy,
    but the Lord takes thought for me.
You are my help and my deliverer;
    do not delay, O my God!

_____

_____

_____

_____

_____

Our prayer gets specific: We are to say, "You're my help and my God, you're my deliverer; let them be ashamed, let them become confounded, let them be confused. As they're trying to scheme against me, you create things that actually cause them to make mistakes." It's not you developing your strategy to accomplish all this, but to trust that God will handle it, so your thinking, your focus, your energy are on the things of life that God has given to you. When I have a problem, I will pray, and then watch what God does. We must trust God and believe He will do as He speaks. This adversity against me is not going to prevail. We can live in that freedom and joy.

Word Definitions: **Covenant loyalty:** continually preserve, guard from dangers
be confounded: be abashed, feel abashed, ashamed
to put to shame: be ashamed, be disconcerted, be disappointed
to be desolated: be deflowered, be deserted, be appalled

How are we to view those who are close to us but coming against us? What does God promise us about this? Why is this important to us?

Read Psalm 41:7–13:

7 All who hate me whisper together about me;
   they imagine the worst for me.[a]
8 They say, "A deadly thing is poured out[b] on him;
   he will not rise again from where he lies."
9 Even my close friend in whom I trusted,
   who ate my bread, has lifted his heel against me.
10 But you, O Lord, be gracious to me,
   and raise me up, that I may repay them!
11 By this I know that you delight in me:
   my enemy will not shout in triumph over me.
12 But you have upheld me because of my integrity,
   and set me in your presence forever.
13 Blessed be the Lord, the God of Israel,
   from everlasting to everlasting!
Amen and Amen.

LESSON 7:
TAKING AUTHORITY AGAINST THE ADVERSITY

_____

_____

_____

_____

_____

Even when those close to us have risen up against us (which is quite a surprise and a disappointment), we follow the whole process. We've forgiven them, we've made an attempt, but they're still rising up against us, which is hard to take. Go to prayer: Father, deliver this, and don't let them have victory over us. Don't let them have effect against us. Don't allow this adversity to continue.

God says, "Watch and it'll happen. I'll do it because it's overcoming adversity. I will show you what I'm going to do. They aren't going to win. You can trust it, and you'll see the amazing things that I can do."

Word Definitions: **whisper:** charm, conjure
lift up: be prideful, come against, enemy will not shout in triumph (victory) over me

2. LIFE DIFFICULTIES / HEALTH ISSUES / SURPRISES:

GET SETTLED ON THIS: GOD'S COVENANT LIFE AND HIS WORD ARE ABSOLUTELY TRUE.

What does God say about His view of the Covenant? Why is this so important to us and our belief about resolution of the adversity?

> **Read Psalm 111:1–10:**
>
> Great Are the Lord's Works
> **111** [a] Praise the Lord!
> I will give thanks to the Lord with my whole heart,
>   in the company of the upright, in the congregation.
> [2] Great are the works of the Lord,
>   studied by all who delight in them.
> [3] Full of splendor and majesty is his work,
>   and his righteousness endures forever.
> [4] He has caused his wondrous works to be remembered;

> the Lord is gracious and merciful.
> 5 He provides food for those who fear him;
>   he remembers his covenant forever.
> 6 He has shown his people the power of his works,
>   in giving them the inheritance of the nations.
> 7 The works of his hands are faithful and just;
>   all his precepts are trustworthy;
> 8 they are established forever and ever,
>   to be performed with faithfulness and uprightness. .
> 9 He sent redemption to his people;
>   he has commanded his covenant forever.
>   Holy and awesome is his name!
> 10 The fear of the Lord is the beginning of wisdom;
>   all those who practice it have a good understanding.
>   His praise endures forever!

_____

_____

_____

_____

_____

As we face these difficulties, we first are to get settled into the essence of God's relationship with us—the basis of His everlasting promise to all His children:

1. God is ever mindful of the Covenant. Which means he's always thinking of, as His basis of operation with us, the Covenant: "I'm going to bless you to make you a blessing, I'm going to bless those who bless you, and curse those who curse you. I'm ever and always processing that as the way of My life with you."

2. God is going to command it. He will command the Covenant. The word command means it's going to happen. As you're experiencing this adversity, He promises that He will resolve it—He will command the blessing that will bring resolution. It is sure.

As you get this settled, and then with every adversity you have, you identify the source and understand the basic remedy to get to the proper place for God to resolve the adversity. Now that you're in the proper place, and are walking fully with God in it, you know that since God promised the Covenant, He will command it to be done and resolved. Why? He's ever mindful of the Covenant, and He's going to command it to be so for us. This adversity is not going to last. It's going to be resolved. Therefore, you don't say: "I guess this is what I have to live with. Whatever happens, happens." See the difference? You never have to say, "I guess that's it." No, it will be resolved, so we are now going to pursue what He promises about this and how He wants to resolve this.

Word Definitions:

majesty: splendor, honor, glory

to be marvelous works: be wonderful, be surpassing, be extraordinary, separate by distinguishing action, to be beyond one's power, be difficult to do, to be difficult to understand

mindful of the Covenant: to be brought to remembrance, be remembered, be thought of, be brought to mind

show: declare, make known, expound

power: strength, might

commanded the Covenant: command, charge, give orders, lay charge, give charge

His Covenant is based upon Him speaking His Word. What then is important for us to receive? Why? How do we do this?

> **Read Proverbs 16:20–22:**
>
> [20] Whoever gives thought to the word[a] will discover good,
>   and blessed is he who trusts in the Lord.
> [21] The wise of heart is called discerning,
>   and sweetness of speech increases persuasiveness.
> [22] Good sense is a fountain of life to him who has it,
>   but the instruction of fools is folly.

_____

_____

_____

_____

_____

Our question to Him is simple: "What do you have to speak to me about this, what is it that will bring about my resolution? What is your Rhema to me—your solution to me personally—which will be based upon the Covenant? You are going to take care of this, so I will go to you to process this so that you can take care of it."

Word Definitions: **word:** speech, speaking, thing

good: (everlasting Covenant): pleasant, agreeable (adjective), agreeable (to the senses), pleasant (to the higher nature), excellent (of its kind), rich, valuable in estimation, appropriate, becoming, better (comparative), glad, happy, prosperous

As we are needing encouragement, what does God promise to give us? Why is this so important for us at this time of experiencing adversity?

Read Romans 15:13:

[13] May the God of hope fill you with all joy and peace in believing, so that by the power of the Holy Spirit you may abound in hope.

_____

_____

_____

_____

_____

In this process, the God of hope will give us what we need—by speaking to us and giving us faith to believe, which is what we need during troublesome times. He will give us the hope about what is going to happen and how it is going to get done.

Word Definitions: **hope:** expectation of good

fill: to make full, to fill up, (i.e., to fill to the full), to cause to abound, to furnish or supply liberally

joy: gladness, the joy received from you

peace: shalom

believing: to think to be true, to be persuaded of, to credit, place confidence in, of the thing believed

power: strength power, ability, inherent power, power residing in a thing by virtue of its nature, or which a person or thing exerts and puts forth, power for performing miracles, moral power and excellence of soul, the power and influence which belong to riches and wealth

BASED UPON THIS BELIEF, WE ARE TO TAKE THE AUTHORITY GIVEN TO US AND USE IT.

What does Christ remind us about authority and the importance of authority? How are we to live this out? Why?

Read Matthew 28:18–20:

[18] And Jesus came and said to them, "All authority in heaven and on earth has been given to me. [19] Go therefore and make disciples of all nations, baptizing them in[a] the name of the Father and of the Son and of the Holy Spirit,[20] teaching them to observe all that I have commanded you. And behold, I am with you always, to the end of the age."

_____

_____

_____

_____

_____

We've discussed that we're living in two kingdoms. We live in the world where this adversity is occurring because of the authority of the enemy, but Christ says His authority is superior. He's created it all, and we're now living in the spiritual Kingdom where He is the king. And now receive it, live it, experience it, and know that we have the power to overcome this adversity and then as we do, teach others to observe that. Pay attention to that life. It's not something to learn about, it's not Bible study; instead, it's something we must experience, something we are to live out – the exercising of this authority in our situations; and as we do, then you will bear witness to others, who also will learn that it is possible that adversity can be overcome. Absolutely. It starts with taking authority.

LESSON 7:
TAKING AUTHORITY AGAINST THE ADVERSITY

Word Definitions: **teach:** instruct, disciple (walk alongside of)

obey: hold fast, pay attention to what I have instructed and given you

How does He send us out? What role does authority play in this process? How do we experience the supernatural and why?

Read Luke 9:1–2; 10:1, 17–20:

Jesus Sends Out the Twelve Apostles

9 And he called the twelve together and gave them power and authority over all demons and to cure diseases, ² and he sent them out to proclaim the kingdom of God and to heal.

Jesus Sends Out the Seventy-Two

10 After this the Lord appointed seventy-two[a] others and sent them on ahead of him, two by two, into every town and place where he himself was about to go.

The Return of the Seventy-Two

¹⁷ The seventy-two returned with joy, saying, "Lord, even the demons are subject to us in your name!" ¹⁸ And he said to them, "I saw Satan fall like lightning from heaven. ¹⁹ Behold, I have given you authority to tread on serpents and scorpions, and over all the power of the enemy, and nothing shall hurt you. ²⁰ Nevertheless, do not rejoice in this, that the spirits are subject to you, but rejoice that your names are written in heaven."

The relationship with God is always the key. We are not to become enamored by Him acting in His supernatural way, but instead, because of the wonderful relationship we have with Him in our day-to-day living.

In this relationship, He says, "I give you the authority to overcome circumstances, to overcome healing, to overcome issues, to overcome the demonic, to overcome stuff that's coming against you. You go exercise it." And the disciples did. And they came back and shared all they saw in the supernatural work. So based upon what God is speaking to us, go exercise this and start to pray against the adversity. Ask God to speak against the specific adversity that you have, because this is His authority of the spiritual, which trumps the material.

Tell God you have this problem, you have this circumstance, and ask Him what He has to say about it. His promise is to help us. Pray for that promise, and you will start to see a change, a resolution.

Word Definitions:

give: bestow, grant, deliver over
power: dunamis
authority: rule, dominion
cure: heal
kingdom: rule, authority, dominion
heal: make whole, restore
subject: obey, yield, submit to
power: authority
all: each and every

What is our role in exercising authority? On what basis? How does it work? What can we expect? Why?

Read John 14:10–14:

[10] Do you not believe that I am in the Father and the Father is in me? The words that I say to you I do not speak on my own authority, but the Father who dwells in me does his works. [11] Believe me that I am in the Father and the Father is in me, or else believe on account of the works themselves.

[12] "Truly, truly, I say to you, whoever believes in me will also do the works that I do; and greater works than these will he do, because I am going to the Father. [13] Whatever you ask in my name, this I will do, that the Father may be glorified in the Son. [14] If you ask me[a] anything in my name, I will do it.

_____

_____

_____

_____

_____

Jesus says we will perform greater works than Him. And this is not greater in nature because: Can you do better than the resurrection? No. He means a greater number. And the reason is that all of us will have the Holy Spirit within us, which means that we're greater in number than He was with His twelve. It's going to be all of us doing these supernatural works by receiving and speaking His authority. We exercise that authority by praying, by speaking, by praying the promises that He gives us against this specific thing. And He says, you're doing the works now.

It's not us alone. It's within His authority that He's given to us. And it should be normal, should be common. And He says: If you pray this way, My Father will do it, who will be glorified by Him performing these works. We will then bear witness to the entire process: that this adversity happened, that we prayed and processed, and we heard. And then it was resolved. It was taken care of by God supernaturally. All verifiable. Who did it? God did it, not us. Why? Because it was resolved supernaturally. It wasn't because of anything we could have done or any skill that we had or some idea we came up with. No, we will look at what God did and will testify to that. It did happen. We didn't put up with it. We didn't just live with the adversity. We didn't accept it or think whatever happens, happens. Instead, we understood that we don't need to live with the adversity. With the Covenant, we can start to live life in a different place. Now, does it mean we won't have any adversity? No. We haven't said that at all. Instead, we said that when we experience it, we must identify the cause of it. Then get the remedy and come to this place where we can say that we are ready to overcome it.

Word Definitions: **work:** business, employment, that which any one is occupied, enterprise, undertaking
do: to be the authors of the cause, to make ready, to prepare, make a thing out of something

LIVE IT OUT AS THE CHURCH DID IN ACTS:

In each of these stories from Acts, write out the important truths about how the disciples were used to overcome adversity. How did they exercise authority and what happened? How can we apply these truths to our lives?

Read Acts 3:2–10; 16:

[2] And a man lame from birth was being carried, whom they laid daily at the gate of the temple that is called the Beautiful Gate to ask alms of those entering the temple. [3] Seeing Peter and John about to go into the temple, he asked to

---

receive alms. ⁴ And Peter directed his gaze at him, as did John, and said, "Look at us."⁵ And he fixed his attention on them, expecting to receive something from them.⁶ But Peter said, "I have no silver and gold, but what I do have I give to you. In the name of Jesus Christ of Nazareth, rise up and walk!" ⁷ And he took him by the right hand and raised him up, and immediately his feet and ankles were made strong. ⁸ And leaping up, he stood and began to walk, and entered the temple with them, walking and leaping and praising God. ⁹ And all the people saw him walking and praising God, ¹⁰ and recognized him as the one who sat at the Beautiful Gate of the temple, asking for alms. And they were filled with wonder and amazement at what had happened to him.

_____

_____

_____

_____

_____

Peter and John are about to go to the temple and come across a disabled person near the gate called Beautiful. He asked to receive alms (money). Peter and John told the person to look at them. He does as asked because he expects to receive money from them. Then Peter said, "I have no silver or gold. But what I do have I give to you in the name of Jesus Christ of Nazareth." And as he took him by the right hand, raising him up immediately, his feet and ankles became strong, and he leaped up. He stood again to walk and enter the temple, walking and leaping and praising God. And all the people saw him walking and praising God and recognized him as the one who was always by the Beautiful gate of the temple asking for alms. And they were filled with wonder and amazement at what had happened to him.

In verse 16, Peter states that this man was made strong, made whole through faith. Faith in the name of Jesus brought about healing and wholeness.

This man obviously had adversity in that he had been sick—paralyzed—for a long time. He was relegated to begging for money. Peter and John say, "I don't have any money, but what I do have is the authority that I can exercise." Did they go off and have a prayer meeting? No. We often look at adversity for us and for others and say: "Let's go off and have this big prayer meeting, and hopefully that works. Good luck. God, would you take care of it?" Instead, they said I have this authority to exercise and overcome your adversity. See verse 16. It's the power of Christ that made him get up and walk. The authority they have they shared to help overcome the problem. And it was the right time. They'd been going to the temple often, and this man had been sitting there each time. That day, though, God said for them to heal him. And as Jesus has told us: I don't do anything unless I see the Father doing and saying it, so in that moment and that interaction, Peter and John were quickened in their hearts by the Lord to respond that way and exercise God's authority.

Word Definitions: **have:** hold, own, possess
strength: made whole
soundness: good health, fully functional
faith: solid conviction (Peter's)

Read Acts 9:32–43:

The Healing of Aeneas

32 Now as Peter went here and there among them all, he came down also to the saints who lived at Lydda. 33 There he found a man named Aeneas, bedridden for eight years, who was paralyzed. 34 And Peter said to him, "Aeneas, Jesus Christ heals you; rise and make your bed." And immediately he rose. 35 And all the residents of Lydda and Sharon saw him, and they turned to the Lord.

Dorcas Restored to Life

36 Now there was in Joppa a disciple named Tabitha, which, translated, means Dorcas.[a] She was full of good works and acts of charity. 37 In those days she became ill and died, and when they had washed her, they laid her in an upper room. 38 Since Lydda was near Joppa, the disciples, hearing that Peter was there, sent two men to him, urging him, "Please come to us without delay." 39 So Peter rose and went with them. And when he arrived, they took him to the upper room. All the widows stood beside him weeping and showing tunics[b] and other garments that Dorcas made while she was with them. 40 But Peter put them all outside, and knelt down and prayed; and turning to the body he said, "Tabitha, arise." And she opened her eyes, and when she saw Peter she sat up. 41 And he gave her his hand and raised her up. Then, calling the saints and widows, he presented her alive. 42 And it became known throughout all Joppa, and many believed in the Lord. 43 And he stayed in Joppa for many days with one Simon, a tanner.

_____

_____

_____

_____

_____

In the first scenario, Peter is there and says, I have the authority of Christ; be healed, and he is healed. In the second scenario, Tabitha becomes sick and dies. Peter is nearby. They call for him hoping he can do something. He comes and finds all these people who are already wailing and have gone to resignation; he does just like Christ had experienced before with people who had given up hope. What does Peter do? He gets rid of them, puts them out of the room.

He then prays: Father, do you want to resurrect her? Yes. Peter prays over her, and she's resurrected. He takes care of that adversity as he was so instructed, as given by the Father. Yes. This is what I want you to do. It's the power, the authority that's given in your life for the situations you face or that you're brought into. It is not up to us. Are you being asked to use His authority? Is God giving you the power to use it? When the answer is yes, then use it. Do not be afraid to use it.

It's the power of the truth that you're receiving and the promise of what you're receiving. It may be immediate as it was in Peter's first scenario, where there was no prayer needed, only a Yes; or when you hear God say yes to you as you seek an answer, do you believe it? If you do, then exercise it, and you will see it happen.

Word Definitions: **heal:** to cure, to make whole
believed: to think to be true, to be persuaded of, to credit, place confidence in of the thing believed

---

Read Acts 16:16–40:

Paul and Silas in Prison

16 As we were going to the place of prayer, we were met by a slave girl who had a spirit of divination and brought her owners much gain by fortune-telling. [17] She followed Paul and us, crying out, "These men are servants of the Most High God, who proclaim to you the way of salvation." [18] And this she kept doing for many days. Paul, having become greatly annoyed, turned and said to the spirit, "I command you in the name of Jesus Christ to come out of her." And it came out that very hour.

[19] But when her owners saw that their hope of gain was gone, they seized Paul and Silas and dragged them into the marketplace before the rulers. [20] And when they had brought them to the magistrates, they said, "These men are Jews, and they are disturbing our city. [21] They advocate customs that are not lawful for us as Romans to accept or practice." [22] The crowd joined in attacking them, and the magistrates tore the garments off them and gave orders to beat them with rods.[23] And when they had inflicted many blows upon them, they threw them into prison, ordering the jailer to keep them safely. [24] Having received this order, he put them into the inner prison and fastened their feet in the stocks.

The Philippian Jailer Converted

[25] About midnight Paul and Silas were praying and singing hymns to God, and the prisoners were listening to them, [26] and suddenly there was a great earthquake, so that the foundations of the prison were shaken. And immediately all the doors were opened, and everyone's bonds were unfastened. [27] When the jailer woke and saw that the prison doors were open, he drew his sword and was about to kill himself, supposing that the prisoners had escaped. [28] But Paul cried with a loud voice, "Do not harm yourself, for we are all here." [29] And the jailer[a]called for lights and rushed in, and trembling with fear he fell down before Paul and Silas. [30] Then he brought them out and said, "Sirs, what must I do to be saved?" [31] And they said, "Believe in the Lord Jesus, and you will be saved, you and your household." [32] And they spoke the word of the Lord to him and to all who were in his house. [33] And he took them the same hour of the night and washed their wounds; and he was baptized at once, he and all his family. [34] Then he brought them up into his house and set food before them. And he rejoiced along with his entire household that he had believed in God.

[35] But when it was day, the magistrates sent the police, saying, "Let those men go." [36] And the jailer reported these words to Paul, saying, "The magistrates have sent to let you go. Therefore come out now and go in peace." [37] But Paul said to them, "They have beaten us publicly, uncondemned, men who are Roman citizens, and have thrown us into prison; and do they now throw us out secretly? No! Let them come themselves and take us out." [38] The police reported these words to the magistrates, and they were afraid when they heard that they were Roman citizens. [39] So they came and apologized to them. And they took them out and asked them to leave the city. [40] So they went out of the prison and visited Lydia. And when they had seen the brothers, they encouraged them and departed.

_____

_____

_____

_____

_____

So, in this city, a girl who had a wicked spirit, was irritating Paul because she wasn't of God. There is truth that light and darkness can't be in the same place. She's even implying something seemingly true, but it is not of God and is irritating because of this spirit of darkness. Because this is darkness coming against him, Paul says, "Enough. Come out of her. Stop bothering us." And because he has the power over Satan, it stopped. So that's it. Did he go off and have a prayer? No. Why? Because Paul has this authority over the enemy and can take it; and he did. And it responded according to this authority—it must flee, and it did. And of course, that causes problems for the people who are making money off of her, and they have him arrested. He gets beaten and is sent to prison. Evidently, the beating didn't affect him much because we know he was singing in prison, and he seemed to be doing fine. God handles the adversity supernaturally by bringing an earthquake to set him free.

And as they received their freedom and release from the adversity, did they stop listening to God? No, they received further instruction the whole way. Even though free, Paul was told to have them come and make it public, not private. So, he made a big deal out of what happened because that's what the Spirit told him to do. God will take care of the adversity, even when we can't imagine how. Who would have guessed that He would send an earthquake? (By the way, during Paul's time in prison, the jailer and his family became believers! There were bigger purposes at work the whole the time.) They trusted in the authority of God all the way around. They took it against Satan. They trusted God to overcome the adversity, and He did.

Word Definitions: **distressed:** be troubled, displeased, offended, pained, to be worked up
command: order, charge

SO, BELIEVE AND EXERCISE WHAT WE HAVE BEEN GIVEN:

What is true about the supernatural? How should we live this out?

> **Signs and wonders are normal and bear witness to the spiritual life. Read Hebrews 2:1–4:**
>
> Warning Against Neglecting Salvation
> **2** Therefore we must pay much closer attention to what we have heard, lest we drift away from it. [2] For since the message declared by angels proved to be reliable, and every transgression or disobedience received a just retribution,[3] how shall we escape if we neglect such a great salvation? It was declared at first by the Lord, and it was attested to us by those who heard, [4] while God also bore witness by signs and wonders and various miracles and by gifts of the Holy Spirit distributed according to his will.

_____

_____

_____

_____

_____

And it was time after time after time these things were overcome because of that power they had. A key is to believe it and exercise what you have. Don't neglect so great a salvation (the wonder and power of God providing solutions, of bringing us to wholeness) as He will bear witness with miracles and miracles and miracles. Overcome this adversity by seeing God and His work, and then know you can take authority against all things!

Word Definitions: **sign:** prodigy, portent, (i.e., an unusual occurrence), transcending the common course of nature, of signs portending remarkable events soon to happen, of miracles and wonders by which God authenticates the men sent by Him, or by which men prove that the cause they are pleading is God's
wonders: miracle performed by any one
miracles: power

How does the supernatural work? On what basis are we to experience this personally?

Authority comes from what is true and what He speaks by faith. Read Matthew 8:5–13:

The Faith of a Centurion

[5] When he had entered Capernaum, a centurion came forward to him, appealing to him, [6] "Lord, my servant is lying paralyzed at home, suffering terribly." [7] And he said to him, "I will come and heal him." [8] But the centurion replied, "Lord, I am not worthy to have you come under my roof, but only say the word, and my servant will be healed. [9] For I too am a man under authority, with soldiers under me. And I say to one, 'Go,' and he goes, and to another, 'Come,' and he comes, and to my servant,[a] 'Do this,' and he does it." [10] When Jesus heard this, he marveled and said to those who followed him, "Truly, I tell you, with no one in Israel[b] have I found such faith. [11] I tell you, many will come from east and west and recline at table with Abraham, Isaac, and Jacob in the kingdom of heaven,[12] while the sons of the kingdom will be thrown into the outer darkness. In that place there will be weeping and gnashing of teeth." [13] And to the centurion Jesus said, "Go; let it be done for you as you have believed." And the servant was healed at that very moment.

_____

_____

_____

_____

_____

In the story of the centurion, he understood that Christ did not even need to come heal his servant. He understood complete authority—that Christ was to speak His Word as authority comes from Him speaking it. We need to constantly ask: What does Christ have to say? What promise did He give us? We will speak that promise.

LESSON 7:
TAKING AUTHORITY AGAINST THE ADVERSITY

Word Definitions: **COME, SPEAK, BELIEVE, UNDERSTAND, AND USE COMPLETE AUTHORITY (HEAR HIS WORD, BELIEVE, AND EXPECT RESULTS):**

understand authority: physical and mental power, the ability or strength with which one is endued, which he either possesses or exercises, the power of authority (influence) and of right (privilege); the power of rule or government (the power of him whose will and commands must be submitted to by others and obeyed)

faith: conviction of the truth of anything, belief; in the NT of a conviction or belief respecting man's relationship to God and divine things, generally with the included idea of trust and holy fervor born of faith and joined with it

We always need wisdom and discernment regarding every situation. We need to understand His bigger story and what else may be needed. Or, we need to understand the timing of His will as to when adversity shall be overcome:

How does wisdom play a role in our receiving His authority to exercise the supernatural? How does it work practically?

Read James 1:5–8:

[5] If any of you lacks wisdom, let him ask God, who gives generously to all without reproach, and it will be given him. [6] But let him ask in faith, with no doubting, for the one who doubts is like a wave of the sea that is driven and tossed by the wind. [7] For that person must not suppose that he will receive anything from the Lord; [8] he is a double-minded man, unstable in all his ways.

_____

_____

_____

_____

Word Definitions: **ask:** beg, call for, crave, desire, require
liberally: simply, openly, frankly, sincerely
faith: conviction of the truth of anything, belief
doubting: to oppose, strive with dispute, contend

As we speak what has been spoken to us, that authority will exercise the promise that He gives us. Then, of course, as we're continuing to process the promise, we will need discernment and wisdom.

We need to ask: "What else do You have to tell me? What can You help me understand? How can I have the wisdom to exercise what You require?" Our exercising this is not automatic. We need understanding and clarity. We aren't to presume anything in our own desire or timing. We are to continue to seek God's wisdom and instructions.

As we have dealt with these different adversities, there is one final adversity that likely will happen and will require a unique response. That adversity is persecution. Let's explore what persecution is and how God instructs us to react to persecution.

What does Christ tell us about persecution? Why is this important for us?

> **Read Matthew 5:10–12:**
>
> [10] "Blessed are those who are persecuted for righteousness' sake, for theirs is the kingdom of heaven.
>
> [11] "Blessed are you when others revile you and persecute you and utter all kinds of evil against you falsely on my account. [12] Rejoice and be glad, for your reward is great in heaven, for so they persecuted the prophets who were before you.

> "... if you're walking in the Spirit, you are living out the life of God with respect, with honor, and you are presenting truth and righteousness."

_____

_____

_____

_____

_____

_____

_____

The word, ***persecute***, basically means to come against you and trouble you, harass you, mistreat you.

Harass you, trouble you, come against you, mistreat you on behalf of something, but on behalf of what? On account of righteousness and righteousness' sake—on account of Him. This is important. If it's true persecution, it has to be on account of righteousness' sake, on account of Him. Often, we hear of persecution justified on behalf of Christianity. But this all comes in the form of harsh judgment. If that comes with malice, with anger, with wrath (people operating in the flesh regarding their attack, which in turn stimulates persecution), this persecution is not for righteousness' sake because it is not of God with His children (believers) acting in a way that honors God, but rather attacking with personal judgment.

Our call is always to live at peace with everybody and to offer that peace in the way that Christ offered that peace. He was always persecuted because of the truth, an offer of the truth. He did not do any of this with harshness or judgment, but he was persecuted. For righteousness' sake.

We will be persecuted. The premise is that if you're walking in the Spirit, you are living out the life of God with respect, with honor, and you are presenting truth and righteousness. And because of that, people are reacting to what you're saying is the truth. They don't like it. This dislike comes from the enemy who is riling them up because it's hitting home, and they don't like the truth. So, what do they do since they don't like the truth, and they're not willing to go to the truth? They attack. They don't attack the truth. They attack you. That's their method, what is the purpose? Silencing you. And it's a matter of how far they can go, including basically imprisoning you. The goal is to silence you. Why? Because you're presenting the truth.

Jesus makes a strong statement: Blessed are you when you are persecuted. This happens for righteousness' sake.

Word Definitions:

persecute: in any way to harass, trouble, molest one, to persecute, to be mistreated, suffer persecution on account of something

righteousness: in a broad sense: state of him who is as he ought to be, the condition acceptable to God, the doctrine concerning the way in which man may attain a state approved of God, integrity, virtue, purity of life, rightness, correctness of thinking, feeling, and acting

insult: of undeserved reproach, to revile

evil: full of labors, annoyances, hardships, pressed and harassed by labors, bringing toils, annoyances, perils; of a time full of peril to Christian faith and steadfastness; causing pain and trouble, bad, of a bad nature or condition

to lie: to speak deliberate falsehoods, to deceive one by a lie, to lie to

What does Christ further tell us about persecution? Why is this element of persecution important for us?

> **Read Luke 21:10–19:**
>
> Jesus Foretells Wars and Persecution
> [10] Then he said to them, "Nation will rise against nation, and kingdom against

kingdom. [11] There will be great earthquakes, and in various places famines and pestilences. And there will be terrors and great signs from heaven. [12] But before all this they will lay their hands on you and persecute you, delivering you up to the synagogues and prisons, and you will be brought before kings and governors for my name's sake. [13] This will be your opportunity to bear witness. [14] Settle it therefore in your minds not to meditate beforehand how to answer, [15] for I will give you a mouth and wisdom, which none of your adversaries will be able to withstand or contradict. [16] You will be delivered up even by parents and brothers[a] and relatives and friends, and some of you they will put to death. [17] You will be hated by all for my name's sake. [18] But not a hair of your head will perish. [19] By your endurance you will gain your lives.

_____

_____

_____

_____

_____

He says: One thing to expect with persecution is that you will be betrayed by those around you. Family members, friends, business partners all could cause you big problems, even imprison you. It could get harsh. But don't fret. Don't worry about it. Don't even get ready for it, and don't come up with a way that you're going to handle it. He will tell you what to say. Let Him help you keep speaking the truth, and do not worry about the consequences. He will instruct you. Do not fear but trust Him.

Word Definitions: **persecute:** in any way to harass, trouble, molest one, to persecute, to be mistreated, suffer persecution on account of something
hated: detested

Christ tells us more profound truths about persecution. What does He say, and what does this mean for us?

Read John 15:18–27:
The Hatred of the World
[18] "If the world hates you, know that it has hated me before it hated you. [19] If you were of the world, the world would love you as its own; but because you are

not of the world, but I chose you out of the world, therefore the world hates you.[20] Remember the word that I said to you: 'A servant is not greater than his master.' If they persecuted me, they will also persecute you. If they kept my word, they will also keep yours. [21] But all these things they will do to you on account of my name, because they do not know him who sent me. [22] If I had not come and spoken to them, they would not have been guilty of sin,[a] but now they have no excuse for their sin. [23] Whoever hates me hates my Father also. [24] If I had not done among them the works that no one else did, they would not be guilty of sin, but now they have seen and hated both me and my Father. [25] But the word that is written in their Law must be fulfilled: 'They hated me without a cause.'

[26] "But when the Helper comes, whom I will send to you from the Father, the Spirit of truth, who proceeds from the Father, he will bear witness about me.[27] And you also will bear witness, because you have been with me from the beginning.

_____

_____

_____

_____

_____

The world is going to detest you as you speak the truth, because they do not want to deal with the truth, as the truth hampers their self-centered way of living. There is a big need to keep you quiet. As they are trying to quiet you, Christ reminds us that they aren't really persecuting you, but persecuting Him; and why should this surprise you? Don't be so surprised that this is going to happen. It will happen. If you've never experienced persecution, then perhaps you're not walking in the Kingdom and sharing the truth of life. Consider then if you are more a part of the world than you are of the Kingdom. This is an interesting test of our walk.

Word Definitions: **hated:** detested

persecute: in any way to harass, trouble, molest one, to persecute, to be mistreated, suffer persecution on account of something

LESSON 8:
ATTACK OF SATAN: PERSECUTION

Paul tells us what happened to him as a believer, regarding persecution. What should we expect, and why is that important for us?

> **Read 2 Corinthians 4:7–12:**
>
> Treasure in Jars of Clay
>
> 7 But we have this treasure in jars of clay, to show that the surpassing power belongs to God and not to us. 8 We are afflicted in every way, but not crushed; perplexed, but not driven to despair; 9 persecuted, but not forsaken; struck down, but not destroyed; 10 always carrying in the body the death of Jesus, so that the life of Jesus may also be manifested in our bodies. 11 For we who live are always being given over to death for Jesus' sake, so that the life of Jesus also may be manifested in our mortal flesh. 12 So death is at work in us, but life in you.

_____

_____

_____

_____

_____

If we are walking with Christ, we will be persecuted. It's normal because you're living in Christ. You will be persecuted. You're going to be harassed. You will be struck down again. Don't be so surprised at it. The way of the New Testament believer is that you're going to be persecuted for presenting truth.

Word Definitions: **persecute:** in any way to harass, trouble, molest one, to persecute, to be mistreated, suffer persecution on account of something
struck down: to cast down; to throw to the ground

As time marches on, Paul tells us the persecution will get worse. What does that mean for us, and how should we understand this for our times?

LESSON 8:
ATTACK OF SATAN: PERSECUTION

> **Read 2 Timothy 3:12–13:**
>
> [12] Indeed, all who desire to live a godly life in Christ Jesus will be persecuted, [13]while evil people and impostors will go on from bad to worse, deceiving and being deceived.

_____

_____

_____

_____

_____

As time goes forward, you who are living godly (in the Spirit) lives, walking in the Spirit, living in the Kingdom of God, will be harassed. There will be deceivers. Expect that. You're going to be persecuted. It's at different levels. What does that persecution look like? Harassment, opposition. People who don't agree with us. They want to silence us in a variety of ways. They try to stop us from doing what we're doing. How can we stop them?

Word Definitions: **persecute:** in any way to harass, trouble, molest one, to persecute, to be mistreated, suffer persecution on account of something
evil: full of labors, annoyances, hardships, pressed and harassed by labors, bringing toils, annoyances, perils; of a time full of peril to Christian faith and steadfastness; causing pain and trouble, bad, of a bad nature or condition
deceive: to lead away from the truth, to lead into error, to deceive, to be led aside from the path of virtue, to go astray, sin, to sever or fall away from the truth, of heretics, to be led away into error and sin

OUR RESPONSES:

As we consider God telling us various responses to persecution, what does He tell us here? What does that mean practically in our lives?

DUST YOUR FEET OFF AND LEAVE.

LESSON 8:
ATTACK OF SATAN: PERSECUTION

Read Luke 10:1–12:

Jesus Sends Out the Seventy-Two

10 After this the Lord appointed seventy-two[a] others and sent them on ahead of him, two by two, into every town and place where he himself was about to go. [2] And he said to them, "The harvest is plentiful, but the laborers are few. Therefore pray earnestly to the Lord of the harvest to send out laborers into his harvest. [3] Go your way; behold, I am sending you out as lambs in the midst of wolves. [4] Carry no moneybag, no knapsack, no sandals, and greet no one on the road. [5] Whatever house you enter, first say, 'Peace be to this house!' [6] And if a son of peace is there, your peace will rest upon him. But if not, it will return to you. [7] And remain in the same house, eating and drinking what they provide, for the laborer deserves his wages. Do not go from house to house. [8] Whenever you enter a town and they receive you, eat what is set before you. [9] Heal the sick in it and say to them, 'The kingdom of God has come near to you.' [10] But whenever you enter a town and they do not receive you, go into its streets and say, [11] 'Even the dust of your town that clings to our feet we wipe off against you. Nevertheless know this, that the kingdom of God has come near.' [12] I tell you, it will be more bearable on that day for Sodom than for that town.

_____

_____

_____

_____

_____

Offer your peace, shalom, which you have in truth. You're living in the Kingdom of God. You offer this truth with gentleness, honor, and respect. Offer peace gently by making a statement or responding to something they might have said. "Would you like to discuss this so we can go into the truth now together?" As they respond to that question, offer your peace. If they agree, what do you do? You stay with them, and you walk them gently through the discussion of the truth, which they could still reject. They could say: I saw it, but I still reject that. Is it our responsibility to persuade them of the truth? No. Can they come back at us and say, "You are an awful person because you believe this"? They can say it. But should that matter to us? No. Blessed are you when you're persecuted for righteousness' sake. The key, though, is how we handled the persecution. Did we start screaming or yelling at them, accusing them of believing the wrong thing? Not at all. In these cases, God asks us to dust our feet off and stop pursuing anything further. Leave this particular scenario. Whatever they say against you or do against you won't really matter. Move on, and don't take the burden of it any longer. Keep offering it to the next person. Stay in freedom, do not worry about this persecution. Move on and enjoy life. Dust your feet off.

Word Definitions: **clings to us:** to glue, to glue together, cement, fasten together, to join or fasten firmly together

to dust off: wipe off one's self, to wipe off for one's self

What does this response say? What does this mean for us practically?
GOD SAYS: "I WILL DELIVER YOU. STAY STRONG, ENDURE, CONTINUE TO BE HONORABLE, RESPECTFUL, AND LOVING. CONTINUE SPEAKING TRUTH; LISTEN UNTIL YOU RECEIVE FURTHER INSTRUCTIONS.

Read 2 Timothy 3:10–12:

All Scripture Is Breathed Out by God
[10] You, however, have followed my teaching, my conduct, my aim in life, my faith, my patience, my love, my steadfastness, [11] my persecutions and sufferings that happened to me at Antioch, at Iconium, and at Lystra—which persecutions I endured; yet from them all the Lord rescued me. [12] Indeed, all who desire to live a godly life in Christ Jesus will be persecuted.

_____

_____

_____

_____

_____

Paul was being severely persecuted. In that scenario, did God tell him to leave? No, He said He'd deliver him from this particular problem. Stay and continue speaking the truth. He promises to deliver us so we're safe. He'll deliver us so it's not going to negate our life, our joy, our full life with Him. It's not going to impact our Covenant living while we're being persecuted, because He's telling us to stay here and keep doing what we're doing. Keep speaking the truth. He's going to deliver us out of any harm that these people are attempting to bring against us. In other words, they're not going to silence us. Even though their opposition may get stronger and stronger, don't let them stop you. Speak truth anyway, because there are people around who are going to be able to hear you and are going to listen to you. And that's what God cares about. God will deliver you from it. In this case, He doesn't say dust your feet off. He says stay and keep doing it.

Word Definition: **to deliver:** draw to one's self, to rescue, to deliver

What does this response say? What does this mean to us practically?

GET OUT OF THERE NOW.

Read 1 Samuel 23:1–13:

David Saves the City of Keilah

23 Now they told David, "Behold, the Philistines are fighting against Keilah and are robbing the threshing floors." ² Therefore David inquired of the Lord, "Shall I go and attack these Philistines?" And the Lord said to David, "Go and attack the Philistines and save Keilah." ³ But David's men said to him, "Behold, we are afraid here in Judah; how much more then if we go to Keilah against the armies of the Philistines?" ⁴ Then David inquired of the Lord again. And the Lord answered him, "Arise, go down to Keilah, for I will give the Philistines into your hand." ⁵ And David and his men went to Keilah and fought with the Philistines and brought away their livestock and struck them with a great blow. So David saved the inhabitants of Keilah.

⁶ When Abiathar the son of Ahimelech had fled to David to Keilah, he had come down with an ephod in his hand. ⁷ Now it was told Saul that David had come to Keilah. And Saul said, "God has given him into my hand, for he has shut himself in by entering a town that has gates and bars." ⁸ And Saul summoned all the people to war, to go down to Keilah, to besiege David and his men. ⁹ David knew that Saul was plotting harm against him. And he said to Abiathar the priest, "Bring the ephod here." ¹⁰ Then David said, "O Lord, the God of Israel, your servant has surely heard that Saul seeks to come to Keilah, to destroy the city on my account. ¹¹ Will the men of Keilah surrender me into his hand? Will Saul come down, as your servant has heard? O Lord, the God of Israel, please tell your servant." And the Lord said, "He will come down." ¹² Then David said,

LESSON 8:
ATTACK OF SATAN: PERSECUTION

> "Will the men of Keilah surrender me and my men into the hand of Saul?" And the Lord said, "They will surrender you."[13] Then David and his men, who were about six hundred, arose and departed from Keilah, and they went wherever they could go. When Saul was told that David had escaped from Keilah, he gave up the expedition.

_____

_____

_____

_____

_____

There are times when God says: "My purpose is no longer being served. I want you to leave. The persecution is going to get worse, and it's going to harm you, so I'm actually telling you to go." In this story, David could have easily assumed he should stay in Keilah. He had conquered Goliath, and he and his men of valor had just conquered the Philistines in the same place. He and his men would have preferred to stay there and live a much better life in Keilah than in caves. Shouldn't he just trust God and believe that he can stay there and also conquer Saul, who is persecuting him? Wouldn't that be a good idea?

But God told him that in this situation, David was to leave. "You need to get out of here because they're going to bring harm to you." David didn't argue. He knew God wanted him to go.

As persecution increases around the world, there are a lot of people who say they are going to stay where they can bear witness; when often God is telling them that it is time to go. His knows it is not safe, and there is no further purpose in staying. There's no universal answer, but if that's what He tells us, if we have a heart to hear, our response would be the same as David's. If God says to go, we are to go. This is one of God's responses to persecution. Our heart is to hear and respond to His will.

Word Definitions: **deliver up:** to shut up, imprison

departed: come out, exit, go forth

For the story of Stephen, what is the final response? What might this mean for us, and how would we view this?

GOD MAY SAY TO CONTINUE TO SPEAK THE TRUTH. YOU WILL SUFFER EXTREME CONSEQUENCES IN THIS LIFE, BUT HE WILL PRESERVE YOU THROUGH IT AND BRING YOU YOUR REWARD IN HEAVEN.

Read Acts 6:8–7:60:

Stephen Is Seized

8 And Stephen, full of grace and power, was doing great wonders and signs among the people. 9 Then some of those who belonged to the synagogue of the Freedmen (as it was called), and of the Cyrenians, and of the Alexandrians, and of those from Cilicia and Asia, rose up and disputed with Stephen. 10 But they could not withstand the wisdom and the Spirit with which he was speaking. 11 Then they secretly instigated men who said, "We have heard him speak blasphemous words against Moses and God." 12 And they stirred up the people and the elders and the scribes, and they came upon him and seized him and brought him before the council, 13 and they set up false witnesses who said, "This man never ceases to speak words against this holy place and the law, 14 for we have heard him say that this Jesus of Nazareth will destroy this place and will change the customs that Moses delivered to us." 15 And gazing at him, all who sat in the council saw that his face was like the face of an angel.

Stephen's Speech

7 And the high priest said, "Are these things so?" 2 And Stephen said: "Brothers and fathers, hear me. The God of glory appeared to our father Abraham when he was in Mesopotamia, before he lived in Haran, 3 and said to him, 'Go out from your land and from your kindred and go into the land that I will show you.' 4 Then he went out from the land of the Chaldeans and lived in Haran. And after his father died, God removed him from there into this land in which you are now living. 5 Yet he gave him no inheritance in it, not even a foot's length, but promised to give it to him as a possession and to his offspring after him, though he had no child. 6 And God spoke to this effect—that his offspring would be sojourners in a land belonging to others, who would enslave them and afflict them four hundred years. 7 'But I will judge the nation that they serve,' said God, 'and after that they shall come out and worship me in this place.' 8 And he gave him the covenant of circumcision. And so Abraham became the father of Isaac, and circumcised him on the eighth day, and Isaac became the father of

Jacob, and Jacob of the twelve patriarchs.

[9] "And the patriarchs, jealous of Joseph, sold him into Egypt; but God was with him [10] and rescued him out of all his afflictions and gave him favor and wisdom before Pharaoh, king of Egypt, who made him ruler over Egypt and over all his household. [11] Now there came a famine throughout all Egypt and Canaan, and great affliction, and our fathers could find no food. [12] But when Jacob heard that there was grain in Egypt, he sent out our fathers on their first visit. [13] And on the second visit Joseph made himself known to his brothers, and Joseph's family became known to Pharaoh. [14] And Joseph sent and summoned Jacob his father and all his kindred, seventy-five persons in all. [15] And Jacob went down into Egypt, and he died, he and our fathers, [16] and they were carried back to Shechem and laid in the tomb that Abraham had bought for a sum of silver from the sons of Hamor in Shechem.

[17] "But as the time of the promise drew near, which God had granted to Abraham, the people increased and multiplied in Egypt [18] until there arose over Egypt another king who did not know Joseph. [19] He dealt shrewdly with our race and forced our fathers to expose their infants, so that they would not be kept alive. [20] At this time Moses was born; and he was beautiful in God's sight. And he was brought up for three months in his father's house, [21] and when he was exposed, Pharaoh's daughter adopted him and brought him up as her own son. [22] And Moses was instructed in all the wisdom of the Egyptians, and he was mighty in his words and deeds.

[23] "When he was forty years old, it came into his heart to visit his brothers, the children of Israel. [24] And seeing one of them being wronged, he defended the oppressed man and avenged him by striking down the Egyptian. [25] He supposed that his brothers would understand that God was giving them salvation by his hand, but they did not understand. [26] And on the following day he appeared to them as they were quarreling and tried to reconcile them, saying, 'Men, you are brothers. Why do you wrong each other?' [27] But the man who was wronging his neighbor thrust him aside, saying, 'Who made you a ruler and a judge over us? [28] Do you want to kill me as you killed the Egyptian yesterday?' [29] At this retort Moses fled and became an exile in the land of Midian, where he became the father of two sons.

[30] "Now when forty years had passed, an angel appeared to him in the wilderness of Mount Sinai, in a flame of fire in a bush. [31] When Moses saw it, he was amazed at the sight, and as he drew near to look, there came the voice of

the Lord: [32] 'I am the God of your fathers, the God of Abraham and of Isaac and of Jacob.' And Moses trembled and did not dare to look. [33] Then the Lord said to him, 'Take off the sandals from your feet, for the place where you are standing is holy ground. [34] I have surely seen the affliction of my people who are in Egypt, and have heard their groaning, and I have come down to deliver them. And now come, I will send you to Egypt.'

[35] "This Moses, whom they rejected, saying, 'Who made you a ruler and a judge?'—this man God sent as both ruler and redeemer by the hand of the angel who appeared to him in the bush. [36] This man led them out, performing wonders and signs in Egypt and at the Red Sea and in the wilderness for forty years. [37] This is the Moses who said to the Israelites, 'God will raise up for you a prophet like me from your brothers.' [38] This is the one who was in the congregation in the wilderness with the angel who spoke to him at Mount Sinai, and with our fathers. He received living oracles to give to us. [39] Our fathers refused to obey him, but thrust him aside, and in their hearts they turned to Egypt, [40] saying to Aaron, 'Make for us gods who will go before us. As for this Moses who led us out from the land of Egypt, we do not know what has become of him.' [41] And they made a calf in those days, and offered a sacrifice to the idol and were rejoicing in the works of their hands. [42] But God turned away and gave them over to worship the host of heaven, as it is written in the book of the prophets:

"'Did you bring to me slain beasts and sacrifices,
    during the forty years in the wilderness, O house of Israel?
[43] You took up the tent of Moloch
    and the star of your god Rephan,
    the images that you made to worship;
and I will send you into exile beyond Babylon.'

[44] "Our fathers had the tent of witness in the wilderness, just as he who spoke to Moses directed him to make it, according to the pattern that he had seen. [45] Our fathers in turn brought it in with Joshua when they dispossessed the nations that God drove out before our fathers. So it was until the days of David, [46] who found favor in the sight of God and asked to find a dwelling place for the God of Jacob.[a] [47] But it was Solomon who built a house for him. [48] Yet the Most High does not dwell in houses made by hands, as the prophet says,

49 "'Heaven is my throne,
    and the earth is my footstool.
What kind of house will you build for me, says the Lord,
    or what is the place of my rest?
50 Did not my hand make all these things?'

51 "You stiff-necked people, uncircumcised in heart and ears, you always resist the Holy Spirit. As your fathers did, so do you. 52 Which of the prophets did your fathers not persecute? And they killed those who announced beforehand the coming of the Righteous One, whom you have now betrayed and murdered, 53 you who received the law as delivered by angels and did not keep it."

The Stoning of Stephen
54 Now when they heard these things they were enraged, and they ground their teeth at him. 55 But he, full of the Holy Spirit, gazed into heaven and saw the glory of God, and Jesus standing at the right hand of God. 56 And he said, "Behold, I see the heavens opened, and the Son of Man standing at the right hand of God." 57 But they cried out with a loud voice and stopped their ears and rushed together[b] at him. 58 Then they cast him out of the city and stoned him. And the witnesses laid down their garments at the feet of a young man named Saul. 59 And as they were stoning Stephen, he called out, "Lord Jesus, receive my spirit." 60 And falling to his knees he cried out with a loud voice, "Lord, do not hold this sin against them." And when he had said this, he fell asleep.

_____

_____

_____

_____

_____

Stephen was killed for his faith, for speaking the truth. Did God tell him to get out of there now? Did he deliver him? No, he went to his death. But we see something about his death.

Who did he see? He saw Christ. He was going to his death, but Stephen, who was being stoned, was speaking calmly: Forgive them. They really don't know what they're doing. He seems to know that he is going to heaven as if just walking into heaven. So, is he experiencing the pain of it all? Not really. We can surmise that if you're called to that point, which he apparently was, then he could remain calm and confident in what was happening. Later, we see Paul being stoned. He was laying there, and they thought he was dead. He just gets back up and starts preaching. He was supernaturally healed immediately and physically was able to preach. He didn't die. We see that's what could have happened in this case. But, for Stephen, he was coming home. God preserved him at that moment, he was not going to feel the pain of this as God took him to be with Him in heaven.

And so now, as you have finished session eight and consider persecution, one question needs to be addressed: Are you presenting truth in this respectful, honorable way? Maybe you're experiencing persecution in your work or your various places of life. What's the cause of it? What's the immediate remedy of it? And then how do you join Him in the authority of overcoming it and start to spend the next weeks processing it so that you can see Him overcome it and ultimately experience the victory of it?

Word Definitions: **power (dunamis):** strength power, ability, inherent power, power residing in a thing by virtue of its nature, or which a person or thing exerts and puts forth, power for performing miracles

wonder: a prodigy, portent

miracle: performed by any one

sign: prodigy, portent, (i.e., an unusual occurrence), transcending the common course of nature, of signs portending remarkable events soon to happen, of miracles and wonders by which God authenticates the men sent by Him, or by which men prove that the cause they are pleading is God's

wisdom: broad and full of intelligence; used of the knowledge of very diverse matters, the wisdom which belongs to men, specifically the varied knowledge of things human and divine, acquired by acuteness and experience, and summed up in maxims and proverbs, the science and learning, the act of interpreting dreams and always giving the sagest advice, the intelligence evinced in discovering the meaning of some mysterious number or vision, skill in the management of affairs, devout and proper prudence in discourse with men not disciples of Christ, skill and discretion in imparting Christian truth, the knowledge and practice of the requisites for godly and upright living

full: filled up (as opposed to empty), of hollow vessels, of a surface, covered in every part, of the soul, thoroughly permeated with, full, (i.e., complete, lacking nothing, perfect)

looked intently into heaven: to fix the eyes on, gaze upon

glory of God: magnificence, excellence, preeminence, dignity, grace, majesty, a thing belonging to God, the kingly majesty which belongs to him as supreme ruler, majesty in the sense of the absolute perfection of the deity

to see: to perceive with the eyes, to enjoy the presence of one, to discern, descry, to ascertain, find out by seeing

Meet with your spouse or friend and work through each of the adversities you wrote that you are encountering right now (those you described in detail on the first day). Then discuss the effect they are having on you. Then process what wisdom the Father is giving you regarding this adversity and what authority the Father is asking you to take toward overcoming this adversity.

CPSIA information can be obtained
at www.ICGtesting.com
Printed in the USA
BVHW022020140621
609534BV00011B/1762